QuarkXPress®

DESIGN TECHNIQUES

For Macintosh

QuarkXPress®

DESIGN TECHNIQUES

For Macintosh

Scott Cook

Michael J. Nolan

Hayden Books
Carmel, Indiana

International Standard Book Number: 1-56830-021-2
Library of Congress Catalog Card Number: 93-80005

95 94 93   4 3 2 1

Interpretation of the printing code: the rightmost double-digit number is the year of the book's printing; the rightmost single-digit number is the number of the book's printing. For example, a printing code of 93—1 shows that the first printing of the book occurred in 1993.

Printed in the United States of America by Shepard Poorman Communications Corp., 7301 North Woodland Drive, Indianapolis, IN 46278.

Trademark Acknowledgments

There are too many trademark acknowledgments to list on one page. To acknowledge every product and every company would require that we double the size of this book. However, because we are environmentalists, and because paper is a valuable (and costly) commodity, we are limiting our trademark acknowledgments to the following statement:

All products mentioned in this book are either trademarks of the companies referenced in this book, registered trademarks of the companies referenced in this book, or neither. We strongly advise that you investigate a particular product's name thoroughly before you use the name as your own.

Published and distributed to the trade by Hayden Books, a division of Prentice Hall Computer Publishing.
For information, address Hayden Books, 11711 North College Avenue, Carmel, IN 46032 1-800-428-5331.

About the authors

In 1990 Scott began his career at Prentice Hall Computer Publishing. Starting as an interior book designer, Scott gained great knowledge of various software applications such as QuarkXPress. With this knowledge, Scott has been able to contribute not only as a designer but as an imprint manager of the production department.

In 1986 Michael J. Nolan co-founded one of the country's first totally-electronic design studios in San Francisco, PRINTZ Electronic Design. PRINTZ's expertise in the design and production of print and multi-media was soon recognized by a large corporate clientele. PRINTZ continues to lead in the application of new technologies.

Michael is currently Director of Art and Design for Prentice Hall Computer Publishing in Carmel, Indiana.

Dedication

This book is dedicated to Juli, Matthew, and Jacob, for without their encouragement and continued support this project would not have been able to be completed.

Thanks also to Karen Whitehouse of Hayden Books for her patience and continued guidance on this project.

Lastly to Jacob, Juli's cocker spaniel, who was a constant companion to the very end.

Credits

Publisher
David Rogelberg

Editor
Karen Whitehouse

Publishing Coordinator
Mat Wahlstrom

Director of Production and Manufacturing
Jeff Valler

Production Manager
Scott Cook

Imprint Manager
Scott Cook

Technical Editor
Juli Pavey

Designer
Michael J. Nolan

Design Assistant
Barbara Webster

Photographer
Don Distel
Spahr Photography

Production Analyst
MaryBeth Wakefield

Proofreading
Diana Bigham, Howard Jones, Beth Rago

Graphics Image Specialists
Dennis Sheehan
Joe Ramon
Sue VandeWalle

Indexer
Jeanne Clark

We want to hear from you

We value your opinions, because our success at Hayden depends on what you think of our books. If you have any comments, no matter how great or how small, we'd appreciate your taking the time to send us a note, by whatever means you prefer.

We can be reached at the following address:

David Rogelberg, Publisher
11711 North College Avenue
Carmel, Indiana 46032

(800) 428-5331 voice
(800) 448-3804 fax

E-Mail:

America Online	Hayden Bks
Applelink	hayden.books
CompuServe	76350,3014
Internet	HaydenBks@aol.com

Introduction

QuarkXPress revolutionized the graphics arts industry. It gave designers freedom from laborious paste-up tasks, enabling them to make layout changes in minutes that would have taken hours or days. Most importantly, it allowed instantaneous feedback on design decisions. Being able to immediately see and refine ideas on screen or on paper is perhaps the greatest advantage of electronic design technology.

QuarkXPress is an intuitive software program—relatively simple to learn. Graphic design and production processes are not as easily understood, and that's where this book is designed to help. The intention here is to bridge the gap that exists between utilizing QuarkXPress and understanding how it applies to the creation of beautiful publications.

This book assumes you already have a basic knowledge of QuarkXPress. It is organized in a non-linear fashion so you can begin anywhere and learn what you need to know. Like Chess, you can learn QuarkXPress's basic moves in a few minutes; it can take a long time to become an expert. It is my hope that this will be a guide for you as you develop and enhance your graphics skills.

x

Contents at a glance

Contents

PART II: TYPE

Contents

PART IV: POST PRODUCTION

This section introduces you to design and production concepts using QuarkXPress. What follows is a wealth of information about the features, characteristics, and tools to create outstanding and provocative designs.

The many components of a publication are seen here in this package.
Designer: Deborah Reinerio, Red Hot Designs, San Francisco
Client: St. Mary's Hospital Foundation

This newsletter mockup, using Lorem ipsum, "greek text", displays the different elements of a typical document. Study the spread closely if you are unfamiliar with layout terminology.

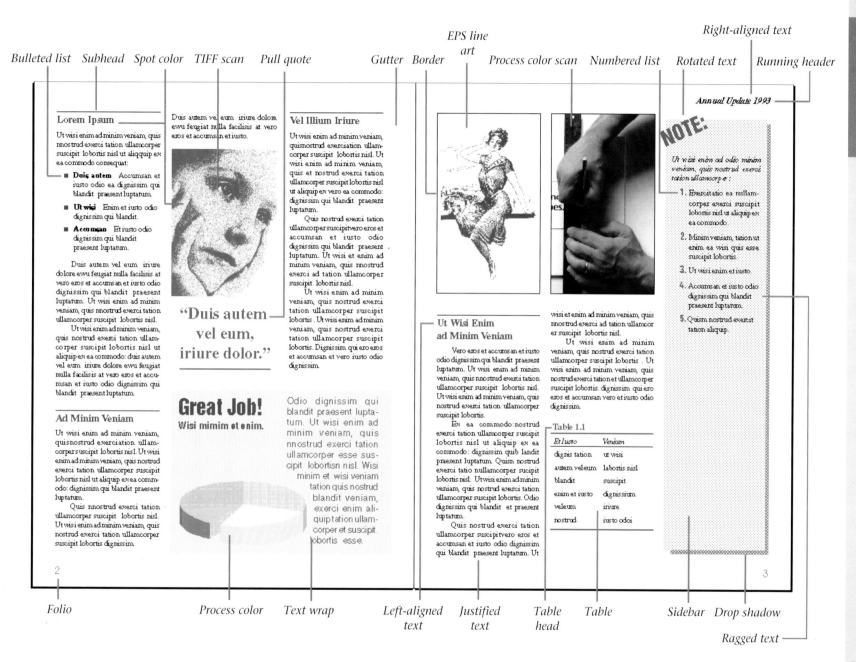

Bulleted list Subhead Spot color TIFF scan Pull quote EPS line art Gutter Border Process color scan Numbered list Rotated text Right-aligned text Running header

Annual Update 1993

Lorem Ipsum

Ut wisi enim ad minim veniam, quis nostrud exerci tation ullamcorper suscipit lobortis nisl ut aliquip ex ea commodo consequat:

- **Duis autem** Accumsan et iusto odio ea dignissim qui blandit praesent luptatum.
- **Ut wisi** Enim et iusto odio dignissim qui blandit.
- **Accumsan** Et iusto odio dignissim qui blandit praesent luptatum.

Duis autem vel eum iriure dolore ewu feugiat nulla facilisis at vero eros et accumsan et iusto odio dignissim qui blandit praesent luptatum. Ut wisi enim ad minim veniam, quis nostrud exerci tation ullamcorper suscipit lobortis nisl.

Ut wisi enim ad minim veniam, quis nostrud exerci tation ullamcorper suscipit lobortis nisl ut aliquip ex ea commodo: duis autem vel eum iriure dolore ewu feugiat nulla facilisis at vero eros et accumsan et iusto odio dignissim qui blandit praesent luptatum.

Ad Minim Veniam

Ut wisi enim ad minim veniam, quis nostrud exerciation ullamcorper suscipit lobortis nisl. Ut wisi enim ad minim veniam, quis nostrud exerci tation ullamcorper suscipit lobortis nisl ut aliquip ex ea commodo: dignissim qui blandit praesent luptatum.

Quis nnostrud exerci tation ullamcorper suscipit lobortis nisl. Ut wisi enim ad minim veniam, quis nostrud exerci tation ullamcorper suscipit lobortis dignissim.

Duis autem vel eum iriure dolore ewu feugiat nulla facilisis at vero eros et accumsan et iusto.

"Duis autem vel eum, iriure dolor."

Great Job!
Wisi mimim et enim.

Odio dignissim qui blandit praesent luptatum. Ut wisi enim ad minim veniam, quis nnostrud exerci tation ullamcorper esse suscipit lobortisn nisl. Wisi minim et wisi veniam tation quis nostrud blandit veniam, exerci enim aliquiptation ullamcorper et suscipit lobortis esse.

Vel Illium Iriure

Ut wisi enim ad minim veniam, quisnostrud exerciation ullamcorper suscipit lobortis nisl. Ut wisi enim ad minim veniam, quis et nostrud exerci tation ullamcorper suscipit lobortis nisl ut aliquip ex vero ea commodo: dignissim qui blandit praesent luptatum.

Quis nostrud exerci tation ullamcorper suscipitvero eros et accumsan et iusto odio dignissim qui blandit praesent . luptatum. Ut wisi et enim ad minim veniam, quis nnostrud exerci ad tation ullamcorper suscipit lobortis nisl.

Ut wisi enim ad minim veniam, quis nostrud exerci tation ullamcorper suscipit lobortis . Ut wisi enim ad minim veniam, quis nostrud exerci tation ullamcorper suscipit lobortis. Dignissim qui ero eros et accumsan et vero iusto odio dignissim.

Ut Wisi Enim ad Minim Veniam

Vero eros et accumsan et iusto odio dignissim qui blandit praesent luptatum. Ut wisi enim ad minim veniam, quis nnostrud exerci tation ullamcorper suscipit lobortis nisl. Ut wisi enim ad minim veniam, quis nostrud exerci tation ullamcorper suscipit lobortis.

Er ea commodo: nostrud exerci tation ullamcorper suscipit lobortis nisl ut aliquip ex ea commodo: dignissim quib landit praesent luptatum. Quisn nostrud exerci tatio nullamcorper sucipit lobortis nisl. Ut wisi enim ad minim veniam, quis nostrud exerci tation ullamcorper suscipit lobortis. Odio dignissim qui blandit et praesent luptatum.

Quis nostrud exerci tation ullamcorper suscipitvero eros et accumsan et iusto odio dignissim qui blandit praesent luptatum. Ut

wisi et enim ad minim veniam, quis nnostrud exerci ad tation ullamcorper suscipit lobortis nisl.

Ut wisi enim ad minim veniam, quis nostrud exerci tation ullamcorper suscipit lobortis . Ut wisi enim ad minim veniam, quis nostrudexerci tationet ullamcorper suscipit lobortis. dignissim qui ero eros et accumsan vero et iusto odio dignissim.

Table 1.1

Et Iusto	Veniam
dignis tation	ut wisi
autem vel eum	labortis nisl
blandit	suscipit
enim et iusto	dignissium
vel eum	iriure
nostrud	iusto odoi

NOTE:

Ut wisi enim ad odio minim veniam, quis nostrud exerci tation ullamcorper:

1. Exercitatio ea nullamcorper exerci suscipit lobortis nisl ut aliquip ex ea commodo.
2. Minim veniam, tation ut enim ea wisi quis esse suscipit lobortis.
3. Ut wisi enim et iusto.
4. Accumsan et iusto odio dignissim qui blandit praesent luptatum.
5. Quism nostrud exerci tation aliquip.

Folio Process color Text wrap Left-aligned text Justified text Table head Table Sidebar Drop shadow Ragged text

Good design requires more than just good taste. The successful designer will learn how to manipulate effects such as color, balance, rhythm, type selection, consistency, and graphics to create an effective and beautiful design without abusing the tremendous power of QuarkXPress. Often the most effective design can be achieved with simplicity.

This leather-bound illustrated history of England (over 200 years old), uses many of the design and typesetting conventions we use today. Columns, initial caps, rules, captions, and headlines were already in use by 1785.

Graphic design has become a common curriculum at colleges and universities only within the past 50 years. The ancient art of typography on the other hand dates back to the 13th century when bronze cast type was used in Korea. Half a century later, Johann Gutenberg awakened the West with his invention of moveable type, which led to the beginning of the Renaissance and Modern History.

The crafts of typesetting, design, and printing have developed a body of knowledge about what works and what does not. Electronic publishing has added to that knowledge, and has given many people the tools that were formerly available only to professionals.

What makes good design is always a subjective judgment. It is easier to identify the reasons why you don't like something than to identify why you do. Nevertheless, when you set out to design a page, think of the following design principles to help make your project a success.

A first rule of design:
Design for your reader, not yourself.

It is said that the best design is invisible. A good design gives precedence to the information contained in the document—without calling attention to itself. Your reader will appreciate your design if it does not get in the way of what is to be read.

There are three goals you should keep in mind regarding readers:

- Attract the reader
- Make your work easy to read
- Motivate the reader to do something

Some designers attract the reader with an unusual or beautiful layout, but fail at guiding the reader through with clarity and motivation. Unless you have a specific reason for making your reader work hard, (and there may be reasons why that would be desirable) make all design decisions guided by this rule.

Much is known about what makes reading easy. Generally, lines of text more than ten or twelve words long are difficult for the eye to track back and forth; as a result, designers utilize columns. Indents at the beginning of each paragraph create a visual cue that a new thought is being introduced. Certain typefaces are easier to comprehend in a paragraph, and others can make a headline catch the reader's eye. Also, there are several tricks for organizing and highlighting text that attract the eye and help organize information.

A second rule of design:
Listen to your client.

Your client is the reason you are designing. If the client is budget conscious, work accordingly. If the client likes red, don't insist on blue—unless you are convinced that it is better. Get all the information you can from the client. Ask questions such as:

- What is the budget?
- What is the time frame?
- Who is the audience?
- What do you want the reader to do?
- Who are your competitors?
- How have you reached your audience in the past?
- What is the existing corporate identity?

Find out what the client wants to achieve with the publication. Determine how to reach those goals. This does not mean that you should give in to every suggestion your client makes. The good designer offers general directional ideas, pointing out what can be achieved within time and budget constraints. More specific design ideas evolve as your project develops.

Electronic design with programs such as QuarkXPress offers the further option of direct participation by the client in the design development. Some electronic designers are comfortable with clients working beside them at the computer. This can facilitate a very workable synthesis of ideas—or it can be disastrous. It also can dispel a client's perception that you just push a button and it is done—like magic! As a designer, you must establish comfortable boundaries.

A third rule of design:

Establish hierarchies and organize your information.

A hierarchy is a series of priorities for your design. Group articles into similar categories that use the same styles for heads and body copy. Choose appropriate sections of copy for sidebars or pull quotes. Some introductory text may benefit from a larger point size or different color. Determine where graphics will best support a topic or idea.

While you organize, be careful not to change the meaning of the copy provided to you. Paul Rand (designer of the famous IBM logo), decries the ease with which electronic publishing allows the emphasis of ideas in copy to be altered by a designer. The designer should never influence editorial content arbitrarily.

A fourth rule of design:

Establish a rhythm.

After you establish a hierarchy with the organization of headlines, subheads, body text, pull quotes, captions, and sidebars—you can begin to create a rhythm. In a typical book, rhythm can be established by the continuation of layout from one page to the next. This layout could include parallel columns of body copy, even or ragged-bottom margins, and the size and placement of graphics or photos—all important for developing page rhythm.

A tool that can help a designer establish rhythm is the thumbnail sketch—a small sketch of where basic elements on a page will go. Rhythm of a layout can be established quickly—in broad strokes and small size—using the thumbnail sketch. One difficulty of electronic page layout is that it discourages thumbnail sketching; the designer focuses on the specifics of the text, rather than the rhythm of the design. Keep the big picture in mind, as well as the details.

A fifth rule of design:

Pay attention to detail.

Nothing affects the quality of the design more than typographical errors or sloppy mistakes, such as rules that don't meet or uneven columns. It always is difficult to see your creation in an objective, fresh way; that is why it is a good idea to have someone else proofread for errors, consistency, and detail in your layout. Just as important is to take the time to run out final laser proofs before sending the file for final output—no matter how urgent the deadline. Skipping this crucial step invites disasters ranging from missed deadlines to a budget destroyed by the cost of extra imagesetting—or worse yet, a job that must be reprinted—at great cost to your client, or maybe yourself.

A sixth rule of design:

Work within your own limitations.

You cannot do more than the constraints of your time frame, budget, or abilities. As the designer, you interpret what is possible within the given parameters. Evaluate your strengths and weaknesses, and design according to your abilities. Illustrate, if you are a good illustrator. Don't attempt to create four-color process artwork if you don't understand how it works. You will be much more successful if you do what you do well, and call in experts when you need them. At the same time, work to expand your own abilities.

A seventh rule of design:
Design for your final output.

Output realities will influence electronic design decisions. For instance, if you plan to use a laser printer to run off 200 flyers, it would be foolish to scan graphics with a high resolution, because the printer can only print at 300 dots per inch. If you are imaging directly to film, you will not be able to physically paste in graphics that have not been converted to electronic format. If you are sending your publication by modem to a service bureau, you must build in the time it will take to send the files, especially if they include complex graphics.

An eighth rule of design:
Involve your printer up front.

The importance of this rule cannot be overstated. You should know who will print your work, the shop's capabilities, and have your questions answered even before you begin to design. The following list is only partial. Each project will involve specific additional questions:

- What are the financial terms?

- When will you need camera-ready art?

- Who is your contact person?

- Where can I save money by making design changes?

- What prepress tasks will be needed for this job? Who should do them?

- Do you prefer film or paper? Negatives or positives?

- What line-screen value should be used for halftones? (Assigned to scans used in QuarkXPress, varying for different printing processes.)

- What color matching systems do you support (PANTONE, Trumatch, and so forth)?

- Will I see a blueline? (Composite proof generated from film negatives.)

- Will I do a press check? (Checking the first few printed pieces before the full run is printed.)

- When will the work be finished?

- What is the rush charge policy?

Good printers are happy to answer these and other questions because they know that planning early pays off. Check through camera-ready art with your printer. It is time well spent. If a project is complex or large, the printer should be happy to talk to you about it before you begin working. You will find out much that can save you time and trouble later. For instance, many times, you achieve better quality if you let the printer make the halftones for photos and strip them into boxes you have left, rather than using scans. This is the kind of thing you may not know if you don't discuss your project with your commercial printer.

Designing with electronic tools, although based on the same concept, is not like using a pad of sketch paper and colored markers. The immediacy afforded by the computer means that design and production can begin simultaneously. There are tools and techniques to emulate the experience of making traditional comps.

Thumbnails

Thumbnails are small sketches designers draw—often on tracing paper—before they place text and graphics into a document. They are a quick composite of an idea, giving the designer a sense of a document's layout, rather than focusing on the specifics.

To emulate the thumbnail sketching process in QuarkXPress, consider setting your page view to the thumbnail setting. It is also useful to print out your page designs at the thumbnail view to prevent focusing on details. You might also use the line tool to represent text, rather than actual words.

Printing thumbnails

Thumbnails in QuarkXPress are different than the traditional preliminary sketches by a designer. QuarkXPress thumbnails refer to printed reductions of several document pages on a single laser page. These can be very valuable when trying to make sense of a large, unwieldly document with many similar pages.

If you are not sure how many thumbnails you want on a printed page, try printing only a few pages of your document as thumbnails. This is because the processing time for printing can be long, and you may waste a lot of time only to find that you chose too few or too many thumbnails.

"Greek" text

Unfortunately QuarkXPress does not come with sample Lorem Ipsum text, text that enables you to place columns of what's known as "greek" text—it is really Latin and semi-Latin—in your sample documents or templates.

A simple way to mimic Greek text is to import the sample text that was provided when you first installed your copy of QuarkXPress. This can be found in the tutorial folder. You can search and replace letters with a different letter of the alphabet. Below is an example using this same paragraph:

> Q simpln wqy to mikic Grnnk tnxt is to import thn sqmpln tnxt thqt wqs providnd whnn you tirst instqllnd your copy ot QuqrkXPrnss. This cqn bn tound in thn tutoriql toldnr. You cqn snqrch qnd rnplqcn lnttnrs with q dit-tnrnnt lnttnr ot thn qlphqbnt.

The main reason for using greek text is that clients can focus on a layout's aesthetics, rather than what it says. Another reason is that often copy is not yet ready for a document and the designer needs to use something as a placeholder. This is the situation where greek text is the perfect solution. Here are a number of considerations regarding Lorem Ipsum:

- Greek text is generally best for body text. You may want to use some typical sample headlines that a reader may find in the publication's final copy. You can go through earlier issues and choose some headlines for this purpose.

- Be careful not to begin all the articles with the same sentence from Lorem Ipsum. This is especially true if you're showing how initial caps can be used; try several variations.

- Pay attention to paragraph lengths when using Lorem Ipsum. Be sure they are irregular. You can do this by combining some paragraphs, and truncating others.

- Greek text does not hyphenate well, because QuarkXPress dictionaries do not include the words in their dictionaries. You can go through your text and type some hyphens arbitrarily to emulate hyphenation and right margins.

Mock-ups

Once you have created the initial design and layout for a document, it is time to make a mock-up. Create the mock-up so that you can solicit input and feedback from others—particularly from your client. It is important that the mock-up have the look and feel of the intended publication. Here are some suggestions for making laser-printed mock-ups:

- If you can, print sides of pages back-to-back by sending pages through the laser printer twice—once for the front and again for the back.

- If possible, use the paper stock that you will use for the publication. You may need to trim it to fit through your printer. You also may need to manually feed the paper if it is very thick.

- If you are printing a color publication, it is valuable to run your proofs on a color printer. Most service bureaus can provide color proofing, from 300 dot per inch laser prints to high resolution Matchprints. If your document is oversized, consider a Megachrome or Cactus print from a service bureau.

- If you are creating a mock-up of a publication larger than 8 $1/2$" x 11", print your pages as tiles, trim and tape the tiles together, leaving crop marks on the outside edges. Align the crop marks for the front and back of the page. Using a spray adhesive, attach the sides to each other and trim with a straight edge and matte knife.

Templates

Templates are just one of the ways you can save a file within QuarkXPress. By saving a file as a template, it can be used over and over to produce other documents with the same specifications. This is very useful when producing books—or any publication that uses repetitive elements. You create the initial design and save the document as a Template rather than a Publication. The next time you open this file, you will generate a copy rather than working on the original. Rename the new file when you save it for the first time. Your template remains unchanged.

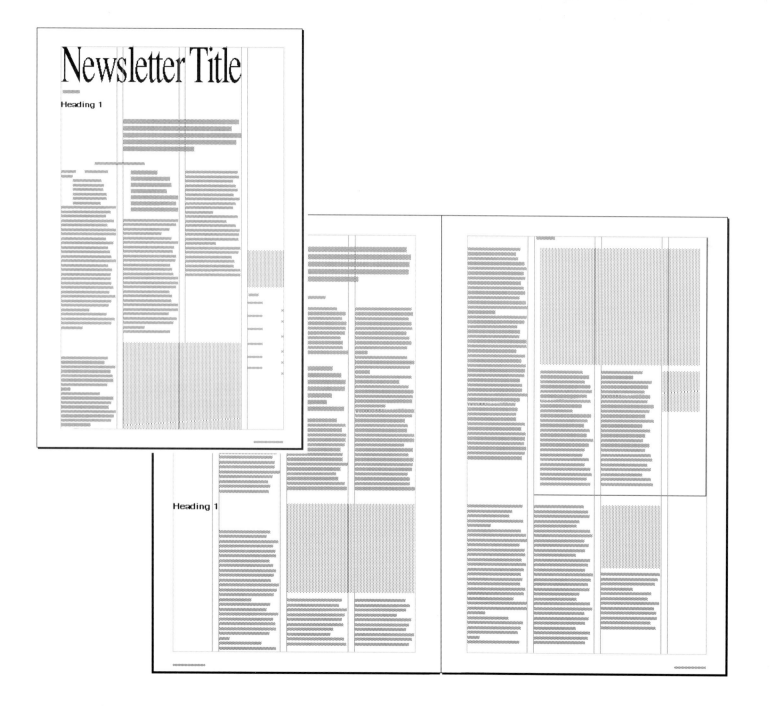

Document types

Different publications can require radically different planning and implementation strategies. This section discusses some basic design and technical considerations for some of the more common types of documents.

Advertisements

With ads, the challenge is to present the most valuable information into the largest space your client can afford. This may mean a full page, or it may mean a tiny one inch by one column format; you may have a budget for full color with page bleed, or you may be limited to black ink. In any case, think aggressively and effectively position your client's message relative to the other ads in the publication.

Design considerations:

- Look at a typical page where the ad you're creating will go. Decide what will make your ad stand out against other ads competing for attention on that page. Maybe the ad needs a strong border or a solid background. Often, simplicity in the midst of clutter will pull the reader's eye to your ad.

- When designing ads for telephone books and newspapers, avoid solid areas of black. Many publications use lower grade paper where dot gain in printing may cause reverse type to fill in. Because of poor paper quality, also avoid subtle tonal differentiations and thin line art.

- Bleeds to the edge of the page can add impact to an ad. Usually bleeds are permissible only on full page ads.

- If the ad's main purpose is to motivate the reader to make a phone call, make sure the phone number is prominent. If the ad is meant to sell services requiring aesthetic judgment—such as haircutting or interior decoration—the ad should be in good taste and very stylish. When selling a particular product, a graphical depiction of the product is helpful.

- Small print is effective only after an ad has caught the reader's eye. Therefore the headline must be solid and strong. Very tight letterspacing or wordspacing, and minimal leading can help reinforce headlines that are read as one strong idea—and also save expensive ad space for your client.

- While white space is important in all designs, you should use it sparingly in ads, because of the cost of the "real estate."

Technical considerations

- Get specifications for camera-ready art-work directly from the publication(s) before you begin your design. Most pub-lications are willing to fax specifications to a designer—or do almost anything else—to make it easy to run ads.

- Because deadlines are critical, verify your due date, the mailing address, and the contact person with the publication.

- Publications are picky about what line screen they will accept. Generally, if the ad is for a newspaper, you don't want a line screen above 90; if it's for a medi-um-quality magazine, 110 to 120 is a safe bet. Higher-end publications can accept 133 or 150 line screen. (See Line screens, page 147.)

- Many publications will not accept paste-up ads, but require that you submit a photostat. If you have composed all the elements of your ad on the computer screen, you can simply send high resolu-tion PostScript output (such as Linotronic paper or film). Some publica-tions accept files on disk.

- If you are creating a four-color ad, deter-mine whether the publication accepts separated film output. In some cases, they prefer to do the color separation for you, in which case you simply provide color photographs leaving boxes for their placement in the film artwork. You also will need to provide a laser print with a low-resolution grayscale scan of the photograph sized and cropped FPO (for position only).

Annual reports

The purpose of an annual report is to show the organization publishing the report in its best light to shareholders or others who have an interest in that organization.

Often, the format is an 8 ½" x 11" booklet. Because of the "image" nature of the docu-ment, good design is essential. Most large corporations retain famous designers for their annual reports, and a lot of the work is in a rather conventional vein. There are those, however, that take chances—like the one shown here.

This annual report features a semi-transparent cover, a simple map, and effective typography.
Designer: Jennifer Morla, San Francisco
Client: San Francisco International Airport

Books

QuarkXPress is excellent for creating books with the addition of XTensions, plug in filters for QuarkXPress. With these XTensions you can have indexing and table of contents capabilities, this in turn makes QuarkXPress a natural for book publishing.

Creating a sample chapter is the simplest way to create a book in QuarkXPress. Once you have created this chapter and saved it as a template, you can flow word-processed text into it and save each chapter with a new name.

Design Considerations:

■ There are standard trim sizes for books. Designing within these configurations will reduce your printing costs, as well as make the book more "stockable" at bookstores.

■ Any book of significant thickness should have a larger margin (or gutter) between left and right pages to allow for binding.

■ Design appropriately for the subject. An instructional book, such as this one, should accommodate multiple graphics and make use of full-color printing; a textbook, particularly for higher grade levels, can be designed for one- or two-color printing. A novel or biography is usually printed in one color.

■ Books need a rigid hierarchy that the reader can grasp immediately. Chapter openers, running headers, title pages, part's pages, and headline sizes—should be consistent and dependable.

■ A serif typeface is recommended for copy that you place in a book if it has any length at all. To use a sans serif would be too much work for the reader.

■ Design books to accommodate reflow. This is what happens when the author or editor makes changes to the text that will result in elements overflowing to a new page. That means various elements should work equally well on a verso (left) as well as on a recto (right) page.

Technical considerations:

■ Books require page numbers. QuarkXPress has automatic page numbering as part of its master pages feature.

■ Use of paragraph style definitions are a given in book layout; without them you may be hard pressed to achieve consistency.

■ Master pages are very important for books. Know how to set up a master page and also how to override master-page elements.

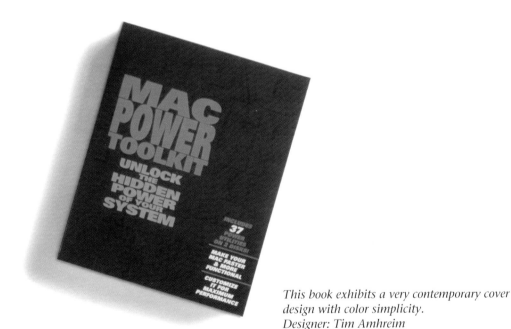

This book exhibits a very contemporary cover design with color simplicity.
Designer: Tim Amhreim
Client: Hayden Books

Brochures

Brochures extend an organization's corporate identity. They can illuminate the organization's goals, or what it sells. Brochures are one of the designer's best opportunities to extend boundaries and be creative because there is often a larger budget for brochures than for other elements comprising the corporate identity.

Design considerations:

■ Brochures should be easy to keep around and should fit into letter-sized file folders.

■ Unless you are trying to project an upscale image of the product or organization, brochures should not appear expensive.

■ Brochures need to be very stylish and can benefit from devices such as initial caps, sidebars, and pull quotes.

■ Brochures should always follow the client's corporate identity program. Because brochures often are presented with an accompanying letter, proposal, or business card, use of logos should be consistent in color, placement, and so forth. Sometimes it is necessary to use a certain typeface in order to reinforce the identity.

■ Brochures should be rich in graphics: graphs and charts, pictures of products and people, or sometimes just a graphical theme should be carried throughout the piece. Brochures must be more than text.

■ Three-fold brochures are an inexpensive and efficient solution. They are made by folding a printed sheet twice. 8 $\frac{1}{2}$" x 11", 8 $\frac{1}{2}$" x 14", and 11" x 17" pages all can be folded to make excellent 3-fold brochures.

■ Brochures must always include a phone number and a call to action, such as "Call us today for a free estimate."

Technical considerations:

■ Color may be used more frequently in brochures than in many other QuarkXPress projects.

■ Bleeds are often possible without extra cost because brochures are usually trimmed.

■ Multiple pages often are part of a brochure—so when creating a QuarkXPress file for a brochure, it's useful to use Master Pages.

■ Brochures often are printed in great quantities. This means that high-quality printing, using metal plates rather than paper ones, is usually more appropriate.

Both sides of this brochure take advantage of three-dimensionality using exciting graphics and color.
Designer: Cindy Chin, Studio MD, Seattle
Client: Printing Control

Calendars

Calendars make great holiday gifts for organizations to give clients. Because they are useful, a company can have advertising in front of its clients throughout the entire year. Each page can carry a new message reinforcing the perception the company wants to create.

It is imperative that calendars be beautiful as well as useful. QuarkXPress is an ideal program for producing calendars.

Design considerations:

■ Calendars should be held together with a common theme. They usually require several pieces of art.

■ The more useful the calendar, the more likely it will be kept; therefore, design calendars that have room on which to write.

■ Clutter in a calendar is very distracting. Simplicity is more important here than in many other types of documents. Try to keep advertising messages to a minimum.

■ Calendars usually follow a standard layout with the weeks in a horizontal format, the days of the week beginning with Sunday.

Technical considerations:

■ Experiment with the benefits of one large text block for the dates versus small, threaded text blocks. This is important when updating the different months in the calendar.

■ Tabs and indents are useful when setting up the number grids.

■ Consider using the master pages for the graphical elements of the calendar grid.

■ Kerning numerals closer together is important, especially when the 1 is part of the number.

This calendar uses a traditional format, and makes innovative use of a keyboard motif for the days of the month.
Designers: Debbie Torgan & Maureen Kane
Client: PRINTZ Electronic Design, San Francisco

Catalogs

QuarkXPress is the perfect program for producing catalogs. Its capability to import word-processing style definitions means that numerous kinds of text treatments for headlines, product names, descriptions, prices, and stock numbers can be applied throughout the document. Order forms can take advantage of tabs and leader.

Design considerations:

- Establish a grid and stick to it throughout the publication. Readers of catalogs adapt quickly to a page layout and expect it to remain consistent page after page.

- Typestyles should remain consistent. Headlines, names of items, descriptions of items, model numbers, and prices should stay in the same typefaces from page to page. Very little can be gained from variation for its own sake.

- Copy should be kept as small as possible, with photographs or drawings of the products featured prominently. (This rule is not always ironclad. For instance, a scientific brochure where the products all look similar, but vary primarily in their specifications, would require larger type and smaller pictures.)

- Forms are a necessary part of a catalog and should be simple to understand and fill out. (See Coupons, page 98.)

- You often see Initial Caps used in catalogs. (See Initial Caps, page 92.)

Technical considerations:

- Text Wrap also works well with catalogs. (See Text Wrap page, 130.)

- Scans are excellent to use in catalogs, and are easy to organize in a program such as Aldus Fetch. You can store them on different disks and drives, and have a ready reference when placing them.

- Photo CD is an efficient way to store a large number of scans, but can be cumbersome when it is time to place them.

- Bleeds can be used as reference tabs and are often used in catalogs. (See Bleeds, page 58.)

The design elements of this catalog are numerous. It combines rhythm, color, balance, with unexpected surprises.
Design: Pentagram Design, San Francisco
Client: The Nature Company

Corporate identity

Logos, letterhead, envelopes, labels, business cards, and signs all contribute to an organization's corporate identity.

Designing a corporate identity—whether for the corner store or a major company—should be approached only after you have gathered as much information about the organization as possible. You should know your client's products, services, market, competition, sales plan, and goals. Once established, a corporate identity should be inviolable. Recommend that the organization create style manual that sets out the uses of the organization's logo, colors, address lines, etc.

Design considerations:

- Design the logo first.

- Make the logo effective in its simplest format. In other words, assume that it will sometimes appear in all black and white. Does it look good that way, or does it require colors to work?

- Make the logo effective when used at any size. Would it look as good atop a tall skyscraper as it does in a tiny newspaper ad?

- Make the logo in equal proportion in height and width. Sometimes it will appear in a narrow space, and if it is too horizontal it will need to appear very small in order to keep its proportions.

- Go for simplicity and timelessness. Use classic rather than trendy typestyles. Make a logo that will last for years; assume that the organization will never want to change it.

- Choose colors that always can be matched. Consider PANTONE or other color matching systems.

- Determine that the paper you choose is a stocked item before specifying it.

Technical considerations:

- Create logo and logotype artwork files outside QuarkXPress, if possible, so that they can be imported and sized as a unit.

- Place artwork for envelopes, labels, and sometimes even letterhead on the same tabloid size page rather than several smaller pages to cut down on image-setting costs.

Letterhead and envelopes

Letterhead usually conveys a restrained organization or company image. After all, letters are as likely to contain bad news as they are good. Letterhead should be businesslike and unemotional.

Letterhead can be beautiful too. Again, design with the reader in mind. Only this time, imagine the invisible part—the body of the typical letter—and ensure that the message is the easiest part of the letter to read.

Design considerations:

- Print letterhead, envelopes, and business cards at the same time thereby minimizing the set-up charge for additional colors.

- Downplay logo, address, and phone number, because most important is the information contained in the letter. (Don't go overboard—make sure these elements are all legible.)

- Specify typical letter layouts so your client is aware of how information can compliment your design.

- Choose paper that is readily available for those times when your client realizes they are out of letterhead two days before a planned 10,000-piece mailing.

- Before choosing a paper stock, make sure there are matching envelopes, even if you are not printing the envelopes.

Technical considerations:

- 8 ¹/₂" x 11" format is standard.

- Check the job when it is at the printer, because most clients are more particular about their letterhead and envelopes than other publication projects.

- Keep careful records of color and paper choices, because clients will always call you for them.

This corporate identity combines the low cost of two-color printing with a modern look. It uses a bleed, a custom designed font, and unusual colors.
Designer: Michael J. Nolan
Client: CDRT, San Francisco

Business cards

Business cards grease the wheels of commerce and have become a cultural ritual in American society. Have you ever met with someone and wanted to send a thank you letter afterwards, but didn't know how to spell their last name? The business card provides instant access, by mail or phone, to the person and his or her company or organization.

Design considerations:

■ Business cards are 2" x 3.5". You will see oversized or undersized cards, but they are unwise because many people file cards in holders or books and the non-conforming card doesn't get filed.

■ Use both sides of a business card to convey information. The back side of a card can contain graphics or other "secondary" information.

■ Phone numbers should be prominent and should include area codes. Complete addresses with postal codes are also necessary.

■ Design for the longest name imaginable in the allocated name space, and for the longest title in the allocated title space.

■ The business card must conform to the corporate identity in every way possible: ink color, paper choice, typestyle, logotype, and so forth.

Technical considerations:

■ The Step & Repeat feature is useful in laying out business cards.

■ Business cards can be laid out 10 up on an 8 ½" x 11" page.

This design takes advantage of both sides of the business card. The glossy stock and dash of the unexpected color draw attention to the company's primary services.
Designer: Michael J. Nolan
Client: Suzanne Clark Productions, San Francisco

Disk labels

Disk labels for CDs, floppy disks, video, or audio cassettes are often an afterthought, but should be treated as part of a corporate identity program. QuarkXPress is useful because disk labels can require type to be set upside down or sideways, and precise measurements are possible.

Design considerations:

■ Type must be very small. Choose a very readable face and stay away from reverses if possible.

■ Pay attention to white space. A label with little or no margin is uninviting.

■ Leave plenty of room for the title of the work and the name of the artist.

Technical considerations:

■ Because type is so small, high-resolution imagesetting is almost always necessary.

■ Lay out as many labels as will fit on an 8 ½" X 11" page. You can print them on self-adhesive paper that comes in many grades and colors.

■ Bleeds can be set up at little or no additional cost on disk labels or cassette covers, since labels must usually be trimmed.

■ Labels for CDs are printed on the disk itself. You can use one to four colors, and preparing the artwork is actually quite simple.

Flyers

Whether for a school play or a neighborhood store super sale, flyers can convey valuable information. Flyers were one of the first document types that desktop publishing impacted. Today they present some of the best and worst designs the technology affords.

It must be that designers think of flyers as the ultimate throwaway. They are usually given little design consideration: often quick-printed on gaudy-colored paper. You find them stuck under your windshield wiper and you go to throw them away—until, what's this, an interesting design? Read on...

Design considerations:

- Although there are few limitations on how much can be printed on a flyer, it is still important to present information in hierarchical fashion, broken into digestible chunks.

- If the flyer is a handout, rather than posted on a bulletin board, consider using both sides of the paper for extra information.

- Consider a color of ink other than black.

- Grab attention with one strong headline.

- For posted flyers, include a row of tear-off telephone numbers or other reminders.

- Dark colored paper makes flyers harder to read. Use good graphics to make flyers eye-catching.

Technical considerations:

- Flyers can be printed in limited quantities on laser printers.

- Because flyers are usually printed on standard size paper, they cannot incorporate bleeds unless they are trimmed to a smaller size.

- For flyers photocopied from high-resolution imagesetter positives, use a line screen value of 85 or 90 for graphics.

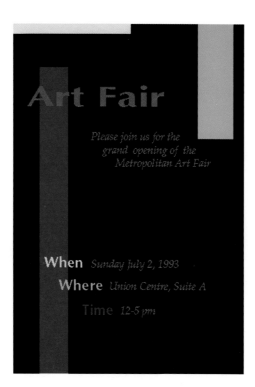

Invitations

Designers usually find invitations a pleasant assignment. The goal is to set a mood for an event and entice the recipient to attend. Invitations can be very traditional, as in the case of a wedding; or offbeat, as may be the case for a theatrical fundraiser. Of course, nothing is wrong with an offbeat wedding invitation.

Design considerations:

- Use a standard size invitation because it will fit a standard size envelope.

- Use an 80# text stock or heavier.

- Bleeds are easy to effect because most invitations require trimming.

- Answer the basic "who, what, when, where, why, how much, and what do I have to do to get tickets?" questions.

- You may need to include a return card and an envelope for it.

- A map may be necessary. Consider a drawing program like Aldus FreeHand or Intellidraw.

Technical considerations:

- Invitations can often be printed two-up on an 8 ½" x 11" or 8 ½" X 14" sheet.

- Crop and fold marks are important because most invitations must be trimmed and folded.

Menus

What a feast for the designer! You have a very special assignment when you are asked to create a menu. Your task is to make the restaurant's offerings look wholesome and delicious—worth ordering. Visualize the restaurant as somewhere you may find yourself some Saturday night. Your job is to make the restaurant appear great.

Design considerations:

- Menus should give the impression of abundance and wide choice.

- Organize with different categories in mind: appetizers, salads, soups, main courses, desserts, etc.

- As a rule, friendly, warm fonts work best with food. Use cold, modern fonts only for austere, upscale places that serve undercooked vegetables in small portions.

- Three-fold menus work especially well.

- Graphics are very important, as is color printing. Ethnic foods lend themselves to thematic graphic interpretations, but try to avoid the clichés.

- If the establishment has a logo, always use it. If not, create one and use it.

- There is a wealth of clip art for menu use.

- A menu that is too slick or overproduced suggests a chain restaurant.

Technical considerations:

- Menus must be durable if used day after day. Print on a heavy stock and consider lamination.

- Make it simple to change the prices.

Newsletters

If you design a newsletter that is so successful it has a 2nd, 3rd, 4th, or 10th edition, congratulate yourself. Not only have you designed a powerful piece, but you have made it so easy to produce that clients just keep coming back for more!

Successful newsletter design and production must be based on efficiency. Deadlines are central to the process. No one respects a quarterly newsletter that comes out twice a year. Unless a last-minute submission is time-sensitive, save it for the next issue.

Design considerations:

■ Generally, a newsletter should not look like it was expensive to produce. In fact, designing for inexpensive printing ensures that you will have the opportunity to design the piece more frequently.

■ A friendly, informal (but professional) tone should be taken in newsletters.

■ Newsletters can be many different sizes other than the common 11" x 17" folded to 8 ½" x 11". For variation, try a 17" x 22" folded once to tabloid size, or 11" x 17" folded twice into a three-fold format.

■ Self-mailer newsletters are the most environmentally responsible.

■ Newsletters should be consistent from issue to issue. Use the same paper, layout, fonts, column headings, and nameplate.

Technical considerations:

■ Often, many people do the data entry for stories. This means you must depend on spell-checking and find/change features found in QuarkXPress to clean up text.

■ Photographs can be supplied by every district office and sales manager in the company. They will be inconsistent in appearance and quality, so take care in scanning and cropping photographs.

This tabloid-size newsletter displays an understated elegance with large type, subdued colors, and restrained design.
Designers: Apple Computer Creative Services & PRINTZ Electronic Design
Client: Apple Computer, Inc.

Newspapers

When designing a newspaper, you should take pride in knowing it will be an important source of information for many people. While you want readers to notice that the paper looks good, you don't want them to be overly aware of the design. Again, the information is the most important consideration.

More newspapers today are using four-color printing as they compete with television and other media for the buyer's attention. This poses more challenges for the newspaper designer, but also affords more opportunity.

Design considerations:

■ The reader is looking for a concise organization of information in a newspaper.

■ Sections should be clearly identified, as should recurring columns and other features.

■ A newspaper needs to look like a newspaper. Find the ones you like the best and see what works for them.

■ Page size is usually limited. Certain formats work with readers and those are what readers prefer.

■ To make it easy for potential advertisers to prepare camera-ready art for ads, use easy-to-measure standard column sizes.

■ Paragraph styles in QuarkXPress must be tightly defined and controlled, or the paper can quickly lose its identity. Desktop publishing means that many additional people will have a hand in the creation and output of the final pages.

■ Justified text is almost a given for a newspaper to look like a newspaper.

Technical considerations:

■ Oversize pages necessitate high-resolution imagesetting, or tiled laser prints.

■ Ads may require physical paste up, coming from numerous sources.

■ Low quality newsprint dictates line screens of 85-90 for graphics.

Posters

Posters are probably the closest publication to fine art. Perhaps that is why you find so many framed and hanging on walls. They are a unique and personal way of advertising.

Design considerations:

- Large format requires thinking big. Make graphics and type as large as possible.

- Color creates impact in posters. If you don't have a big budget for printing, use colored paper and one or two ink colors.

- When you think about designing a poster, think drama.

Technical considerations:

- Since posters often are collected and displayed long after the event they advertise, use good quality paper for printing them.

- If you start with original art that is very small and use it for scanned graphics in the poster, flaws will be exaggerated.

The poster shown here relies on bold graphics and a striking positive/negative interplay to capture attention.
Designer: Jennifer Morla, San Francisco
Client: Capp Street Project

Programs

Programs for events often change at the last minute. Whether for small community groups or expositions, a program must communicate immediacy. It is a snapshot in time: this event, this date. Programs always invite the designer to experiment, be playful and break the boundaries.

Design considerations:

■ Most theatrical and other groups need to keep costs down, and therefore programs should be straightforward and efficient to print.

■ Because most programs include ads, the page layout must accommodate them.

■ Photos of actors or other participants add interest and life to a program.

■ Programs follow fairly rigid formats, from their (typical) 5 ¹/₂" x 8 ¹/₂" size, to their progression of information.

■ Graphics are essential for program covers, and also liven up interiors.

The video expostion program below shows many of the elements found in programs, such as schedules and registration information. Created within a small budget, it uses two colors: a metallic and black ink.
Designer: Michael J. Nolan
Client: Knowledge Industries, Inc.

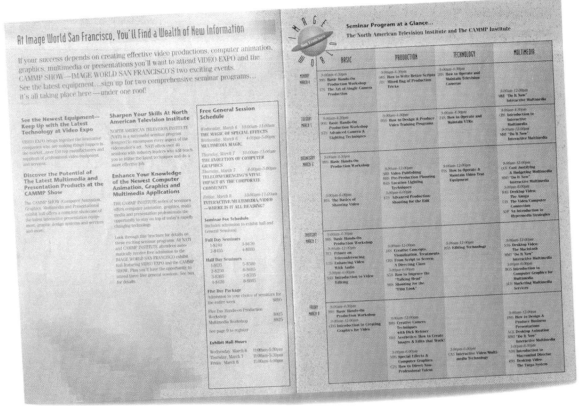

Resumes

The desktop production of resumes has changed the way people look for jobs. Savvy job hunters now know that nothing less than a typeset, laser-printed resume on quality paper stock will do.

Of course, the design of a resume depends on the kind of job sought. An accountant should have a very different looking resume from that of an actor. If there is any doubt about which way to go, the rule is simple: straightforward and free from adornment.

Design considerations:

■ The average resume is given about 15 seconds consideration by its recipient. Design accordingly.

■ Use more than one column to "beef up" paragraphs. One or two lines of text across an entire page will take up three or four lines on a half-page column. This makes the applicant's accomplishments look meatier.

■ Create an aura of class, accomplishment, and sophistication for your client.

■ Use bullet points wherever possible.

■ Avoid abbreviations for states, titles, and other categories.

Technical considerations:

■ Most clients want adaptability for changing job objectives, and easy updating of a resume. Make it easy to change.

■ Most resumes will be laser printed. Choose a paper stock that looks good with laser-quality type, and avoid graphics which require high resolution to look good.

Document parts

There are certain elements that many publications have in common—financial tables, nameplates, mastheads, sidebars—and the style in which these elements are treated must be consistent with the purpose and appearance of the document of which they are a part.

Covers

Books, magazines, and annual reports always have covers. Brochures, even if they are constructed from a three-fold sheet, have a section that serves as a cover; other documents have no cover. Covers fall into two categories: those that sell, and those that protect. Some covers do both.

Covers that sell

Books and magazines usually depend on their packaging to sell. They must observe some or all of the following conventions:

- Covers usually contain numerous elements: title, subtitle, author, bullet copy, volume numbers, dates, illustrations, etc. It is crucial that these elements relate to one another. Creating a grid will make this much easier.

- Place the title near the top, in a strong typeface.

- Make sure that the color of any text appearing on the cover contrasts with the illustration behind it, so that it can be read easily.

- If there is subsidiary information—such as a subtitle or text describing topics covered inside—it should be strongly styled.

- Text on a multi-colored background may make uniform contrast difficult. Consider a drop shadow behind the text to make it stand out against the different shades.

- Spend more resources (design time and printing budget) on the cover than the interior. This should yield a greater number of readers for the publication. It is not uncommon for publications with a one-color interior to have four-color covers.

- Strive for unity between the cover and the interior. This can be achieved by using the same typefaces and colors, or by displaying illustrations or photos from the inside of the publication on the cover.

- The spine of a book is considered as important as its front cover—because books are often displayed spine-out in stores. The only way to capture the buyer's eye is often with a thin strip of effective color and typography.

Covers that protect

Protecting the interior pages is another function of covers, particularly if the publication is being mailed. That's why the trade name for heavy paper is "cover stock." Here are some considerations about printing on heavy stock:

- Folding heavy stock requires scoring so that the paper does not "break" along the fold.

- Most paper stock that may be used for the interior pages of a document can be matched in a cover stock (80# or more). If you are using, for instance, a recycled, speckletone ivory stock for interior pages, either match it exactly in cover stock, or use a contrasting color in the same stock.

Mastheads

Mastheads—found in newsletters, magazines and similar publications—are usually narrow columns on the table of contents page containing information such as editors' and the publisher's names, the organization's name and address, volume and issue numbers, etc. Their characteristics are as follows:

- Small type is usually used in mastheads. If you are using larger than eight point type, it is probably too large.

- Mastheads should not be more than a column wide, and seldom more than half a page in height.

- Mastheads can be set off by rules around them. They should not be a major graphic element, and usually do not call attention to themselves.

The cover to the left is a folder used to contain a brochure and data sheets. It is printed two-color on an 80# buff colored paper.
Designer: Mike Bertoni, PRINTZ Electronic Design, San Francisco.
Client: California Cable Television Association

Nameplates

Nameplates, which are the identifying title of a newsletter or magazine, are one of the most important design elements in those publications because they give the reader a visual cue about what the document is.

Because the nameplate is the primary identification for your publication, it must convey the proper "attitude." Depending on the purpose of the document, it should be dignified, humorous, corporate, avant garde, childlike, old-fashioned, contemporary, reassuring, or upsetting. Here are some guidelines for designing nameplates:

■ Spend time designing the nameplate because it will be used with each issue, and once established, should not change.

■ Use strong typography and pay careful attention to the hierarchies. The name of the publication is more important than the volume or issue number.

■ Make the name of the publication as large as possible; you can even increase the size of the text by few points after kerning the letters very tightly together. Downplay small words such as "The."

■ If possible, create the nameplate in a graphics program such as Aldus FreeHand or Adobe Illustrator, because this enables you to import it into QuarkXPress as one object that you can copy and reduce for other pages.

■ Taglines such as "A Quarterly Newsletter from Organization X" are important to help the reader identify what is being presented.

■ If you want a lot of color in a publication, use color in the nameplate, and print enough shells (preprinted blank pages for all the issues you intend to publish) for the next year. This way, you can print the text and graphics for the succeeding issues in one or two colors, and only incur the setup charges for the nameplate colors one time. The disadvantage is that your printer has to store the shells, and your client has to pay for all the paper up front. An advantage is that it commits your client to future issues.

■ Make sure you relate the nameplate to the column format that appears below it—even if it spans all the columns. If you have a three-column format, perhaps one part of the nameplate spans one column, and another part is two columns wide.

■ If you are going to use the name of the month(s) to identify issues, design with "September/October" to determine the maximum amount of space you will need for future months.

■ Type placed vertically makes interesting nameplates.

Sidebars

Sidebars, which are related stories set aside from other text with a special font or graphic treatment, serve as another "point of entry" into an article or page. Many times they are complete "stories" unto themselves, giving the reader a synopsis of the information that may be the only text read. Often, sidebars contain graphs, charts, or other visual information besides text. Sometimes, an entire article can be treated as a sidebar. Discovering a well-designed sidebar on a page gives the reader a feeling of sharing "a secret" by being privy to special information.

- If a sidebar is primarily text, it is usually effective from a design standpoint to put it in a different font, or to use a different color for the type. This treatment is less common than the simple screened box which is often used.

- A sidebar bleeding off the edge of the page can be very effective, particularly if you use a create a gradient screen in a program such as Aldus Freehand or Adobe Illustrator and import it.

- If a sidebar fills a normal column, the text or graphics inside it should be narrower than that in columns, so that they have margins within the sidebar.

- Sidebars are a good way to set up a table of contents on the front page of a newsletter. Use a heading such as "In this Issue" in a stylish type treatment.

Table of contents

Building a table of contents (TOC) for a book at one time was a laborious process—with great potential for accidentally listing a wrong page number if pages were changed. With the addition of Sonar TOC by Virginia Systems, a Quark XTension, this problem has been solved, making it possible to create a table of contents for one or even several different files at once. Here is how it is done:

1. Decide whether to create a separate publication for a table of contents, or if it will go on a page of your current document. If you choose to have a separate publication, you will need to generate a separate template.

2. Determine which headings, (chapter names, subheads, etc.), you are going to list in your table of contents.

3. Sonar TOC is based upon a paragraph attribute setting. You can easily apply this attribute to styles.

4. Select Sonar TOC from the Utilities menu, and double-click on a style for the paragraph you want to include in the table of contents.

5. Check Include in the table of contents.

6. Repeat steps 4 and 5 for other styles that should be included in the TOC.

7. Close the dialog box.

8. Choose Create TOC, and select the settings you want; click on the OK button.

9. Format the table of contents with the correct type, indent, and tabbing specifications. Style definitions are automatically generated for the tables of contents. It is best to change text formatting by changing those style definitions.

Tables

Tables can be challenging because they require extensive use of tabs, small point sizes, rules, reverses, headings, and other difficult elements. Tables often don't fit into columns; and are hard to make look good.

Tables are an important part of many publications, and can be simple and elegant. Once again, QuarkXPress contains the kind of powerful features that can make tables easy.

■ Designing tables

Whether for a service schedule, such as the one shown here, or for a financial report, information must be easy for the reader to find quickly. If there are numerous rows and columns, try differentiating them visually. You can use screens or rules to do this.

Lay out the text in your table before attempting to create screened backgrounds or rules to divide the columns. Use the longest word or number to determine the width of columns, and if you can, make the column widths equal. If they are, you will be able to use the Multiple paste feature to space them equally across the page.

Table headings should look different than the rest of the information. Try reverse text in a solid bar, or an italic typeface to differentiate them. If using horizontal rules, the one between the headings and the body of information may look best if it is a different weight or color than the other rules.

■ Tabbing

Correctly set tabs are the backbone of a well-constructed table. If you are using numbers, consider whether the tabs should be decimal or centered; rarely will they be left or right hand tabs. (See Indents/tabs on page 96.)

■ Importing tables

When you import tables from other programs such as Microsoft Excel, they should be saved as tab-delimited text when exported. This means that each column is separated by tabs, and each row by returns, making it easy to format the imported table using the Indents/tabs feature.

If text does not appear neatly in columns when you import a tab-delimited table, you may need to select the entire text block, select the tabs option under the format menu, and set the individual tabs farther apart. Another way to solve this problem would be to decrease the point size of the text.

■ Creating fractions

Tables usually contain numerals, and numerals often contain fractions. It is not typographically correct to make a fraction that reads 1/2; better that it should read $^1/_2$. You can set up your type specifications to create a fraction like this. Here is how:

1. Select the first number of the fraction, reduce it by 2 points, and change it to reflect the changes shown on the measurements palette below.

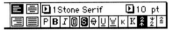

2. Then select the last number of the fraction, reduce it by 2 points, and change it to reflect that of the second figure.

This table example is from a shipping company's service schedule. Note how its columns and rows are differentiated by color and lines.
Designer: Jim Andrews, Redwood City, CA
Client: American President Companies

From North Atlantic, Midwest, East Canada

DEPARTS

VESSEL VOYAGE NO.	POLK 21 POK	ROOSEVELT 67 FDR	ADAMS 29 ADM	MONROE 82 MON	JACKSON 30 JAX	EISENHOWER 69 IKE	TRUMAN 34 TRM	WASHINGTON 83 WAS		KENNEDY 32 JFK	LINCOLN 85 LIN	POLK 32 POK	ROOSEVELT 68 FDR	ADAMS 30 ADM	MONROE 83 MON	JACKSON 31 JAX	EISENHOWER 70 IKE	TRUMAN 35 TRM	WASHINGTON 84 WAS	KENNEDY 33 JFK	LINCOLN 86 LIN
New York/New Jersey	6-24	6-26	7-1	7-3	7-8	7-10	7-15	7-17		7-22	7-24	7-29	7-31	8-5	8-7	8-12	8-14	8-19	8-21	8-26	8-28
Baltimore	6-24	6-26	7-1	7-3	7-8	7-10	7-15	7-17		7-22	7-24	7-29	7-31	8-5	8-7	8-12	8-14	8-19	8-21	8-26	8-28
Boston	6-24	6-26	7-1	7-3	7-8	7-10	7-15	7-17		7-22	7-24	7-29	7-31	8-5	8-7	8-12	8-14	8-19	8-21	8-26	8-28
Philadelphia	6-23	6-26	6-30	7-3	7-7	7-10	7-14	7-17		7-21	7-24	7-28	7-31	8-4	8-7	8-11	8-14	8-18	8-21	8-25	8-28
Montreal	6-21	6-21	6-28	6-28	7-5	7-5	7-12	7-12		7-19	7-19	7-26	7-26	8-2	8-2	8-9	8-9	8-16	8-16	8-23	8-23
Toronto	6-21	6-21	6-28	6-28	7-5	7-5	7-12	7-12		7-19	7-19	7-26	7-26	8-2	8-2	8-9	8-9	8-16	8-16	8-23	8-23
Memphis	6-23	6-28	6-30	7-7	7-7	7-12	7-14	7-19		7-21	7-26	7-28	8-2	8-4	8-9	8-11	8-16	8-18	8-23	8-25	8-30
Chicago	6-26	6-28	7-3	7-5	7-10	7-12	7-17	7-19		7-24	7-26	7-31	8-2	8-7	8-9	8-14	8-16	8-21	8-23	8-28	8-30
Detroit	6-25	6-27	7-2	7-4	7-9	7-11	7-16	7-18		7-23	7-25	7-30	8-1	8-6	8-8	8-13	8-15	8-20	8-22	8-27	8-29
Cincinnati	6-25	6-27	7-2	7-4	7-9	7-11	7-16	7-18		7-23	7-25	7-30	8-1	8-6	8-8	8-13	8-15	8-20	8-22	8-27	8-29
Kansas City	6-25	6-27	7-2	7-4	7-9	7-11	7-16	7-18		7-23	7-25	7-30	8-1	8-6	8-8	8-13	8-15	8-20	8-22	8-27	8-29
St. Louis	6-25	6-27	7-2	7-4	7-9	7-11	7-16	7-18		7-23	7-25	7-30	8-1	8-6	8-8	8-13	8-15	8-20	8-22	8-27	8-29
San Pedro	7-2	7-3	7-9	7-10	7-16	7-17	7-23	7-24		7-30	7-31	8-6	8-7	8-13	8-14	8-20	8-21	8-27	8-28	9-3	9-4
Oakland	7-4	7-4	7-11	7-11	7-18	7-18	7-25	7-25		8-1	8-1	8-8	8-8	8-15	8-15	8-22	8-22	8-29	8-29	9-5	9-5

ARRIVES

VESSEL VOYAGE NO.	POLK 21 POK	ROOSEVELT 67 FDR	ADAMS 29 ADM	MONROE 82 MON	JACKSON 30 JAX	EISENHOWER 69 IKE	TRUMAN 34 TRM	WASHINGTON 83 WAS		KENNEDY 32 JFK	LINCOLN 85 LIN	POLK 32 POK	ROOSEVELT 68 FDR	ADAMS 30 ADM	MONROE 83 MON	JACKSON 31 JAX	EISENHOWER 70 IKE	TRUMAN 35 TRM	WASHINGTON 84 WAS	KENNEDY 33 JFK	LINCOLN 86 LIN
Japan, Korea, Hong Kong, China, Taiwan, Philippines, Guam																					
Yokohama	7-15		7-22		7-29		8-5			8-12		8-19		8-26		9-2		9-9		9-16	
Tokyo	7-16		7-23		7-30		8-6			8-13		8-20		8-27		9-3		9-10		9-17	
Nagoya	7-18		7-25		8-1		8-8			8-15		8-22		8-29		9-5		9-12		9-19	
Shimizu	7-16		7-23		7-30		8-6			8-13		8-20		8-27		9-3		9-10		9-17	
Kobe/Osaka	7-16		7-23		7-30		8-6			8-13		8-20		8-27		9-3		9-10		9-17	
Okinawa	7-29	7-22	8-5	8-5	8-12	8-12	8-19	8-19		8-26	8-26	9-2	9-2	9-9	9-9	9-16	9-16	9-23	9-23	9-30	9-30
Busan/Incheon	7-21		7-28		8-4		8-11			8-18		8-25		9-1		9-8		9-15		9-22	
Keelung	7-21	7-22	7-28	7-29	8-4	8-5	8-11	8-12		8-18	8-19	8-25	8-26	9-1	9-2	9-8	9-9	9-15	9-16	9-22	9-23
Kaohsiung	7-19	7-20	7-26	7-27	8-2	8-3	8-9	8-10		8-16	8-17	8-23	8-24	8-30	8-31	9-6	9-7	9-13	9-14	9-20	9-21
Hwangpu	7-27	7-27	8-3	8-3	8-10	8-10	8-17	8-17		8-24	8-24	8-31	8-31	9-7	9-7	9-14	9-14	9-21	9-21	9-28	9-28
Chiwan	7-28	7-28	8-4	8-4	8-11	8-11	8-18	8-18		8-25	8-25	9-1	9-1	9-8	9-8	9-15	9-15	9-22	9-22	9-29	9-29
Hong Kong	7-26	7-25	8-1	8-1	8-8	8-8	8-10	8-15		8-17	8-22	8-24	8-29	8-31	9-5	9-7	9-12	9-14	9-19	9-21	9-26
Manila	7-25	7-25	8-1	8-1	8-8	8-8	8-15	8-15		8-22	8-22	8-29	8-29	9-5	9-5	9-12	9-12	9-19	9-19	9-26	9-26
Guam/Saipan			7-22		7-29		8-5			8-12		8-19		8-26		9-2		9-9		9-16	
Singapore, Malaysia, Indonesia, Thailand, Bangladesh																					
Singapore	7-25	7-25	8-1	8-1	8-8	8-8	8-15	8-15		8-22	8-22	8-29	8-29	9-5	9-5	9-12	9-12	9-19	9-19	9-26	9-26
Penang	8-1	8-1	8-8	8-8	8-15	8-15	8-22	8-22		8-29	8-29	9-5	9-5	9-12	9-12	9-19	9-19	9-26	9-26	10-3	10-3
Pt. Klang	7-30	7-30	8-6	8-6	8-13	8-13	8-20	8-20		8-27	8-27	9-3	9-3	9-10	9-10	9-17	9-17	9-24	9-24	10-1	10-1
Jakarta	8-2	8-2	8-9	8-9	8-16	8-16	8-23	8-23		8-30	8-30	9-6	9-6	9-13	9-13	9-20	9-20	9-27	9-27	10-4	10-4
Surabaya	7-31	7-31	8-7	8-7	8-14	8-14	8-21	8-21		8-28	8-28	9-4	9-4	9-11	9-11	9-18	9-18	9-25	9-25	10-2	10-2
Bangkok	7-29	7-29	8-5	8-5	8-12	8-12	8-19	8-19		8-26	8-26	9-2	9-2	9-9	9-9	9-16	9-16	9-23	9-23	9-30	9-30
Chittagong	8-1	8-1	8-8	8-8	8-15	8-15	8-22	8-22		8-29	8-29	9-5	9-5	9-12	9-12	9-19	9-19	9-26	9-26	10-3	10-3
India, Pakistan, Middle East, Sri Lanka																					
Bombay	8-10	8-10	8-17	8-17	8-24	8-24	8-31	8-31		9-7	9-7	9-14	9-14	9-21	9-21	9-28	9-28	10-5	10-5	10-12	10-12
Cochin	8-1	8-1	8-8	8-8	8-15	8-15	8-22	8-22		8-29	8-29	9-5	9-5	9-12	9-12	9-19	9-19	9-26	9-26	10-3	10-3
Madras	8-1	8-1	8-8	8-8	8-15	8-15	8-22	8-22		8-29	8-29	9-5	9-5	9-12	9-12	9-19	9-19	9-26	9-26	10-3	10-3
Calcutta	8-2	8-2	8-9	8-9	8-16	8-16	8-23	8-23		8-30	8-30	9-6	9-6	9-13	9-13	9-20	9-20	9-27	9-27	10-4	10-4
Karachi	8-5	8-5	8-12	8-12	8-19	8-19	8-26	8-26		9-2	9-2	9-9	9-9	9-16	9-16	9-23	9-23	9-30	9-30	10-7	10-7
Muscat	8-4	8-4			8-18	8-18				9-1	9-1			9-15	9-15			9-29	9-29		
Dammam	8-9	8-9	8-16	8-16	8-23	8-23	8-30	8-30		9-6	9-6	9-13	9-13	9-20	9-20	9-27	9-27	10-4	10-4	10-11	10-11
Kuwait	8-12	8-12	8-19	8-19	8-26	8-26	9-2	9-2		9-9	9-9	9-16	9-16	9-23	9-23	9-30	9-30	10-7	10-7	10-14	10-14
Bahrain	8-8	8-8	8-15	8-15	8-22	8-22	8-29	8-29		9-5	9-5	9-12	9-12	9-19	9-19	9-26	9-26	10-3	10-3	10-10	10-10
Riyadh	8-13	8-13	8-20	8-20	8-27	8-27	9-3	9-3		9-10	9-10	9-17	9-17	9-24	9-24	10-1	10-1	10-8	10-8	10-15	10-15
Doha/Sharjah/Abu Dhabi	8-4	8-4	8-11	8-11	8-18	8-18	8-25	8-25		9-1	9-1	9-8	9-8	9-15	9-15	9-22	9-22	9-29	9-29	10-6	10-6
Fujairah/Jebel Ali	8-2	8-2	8-9	8-9	8-16	8-16	8-23	8-23		8-30	8-30	9-6	9-6	9-13	9-13	9-20	9-20	9-27	9-27	10-4	10-4
Dubai	8-3	8-3	8-10	8-10	8-17	8-17	8-24	8-24		8-31	8-31	9-7	9-7	9-14	9-14	9-21	9-21	9-28	9-28	10-5	10-5
Colombo	7-29	7-29	8-5	8-5	8-12	8-12	8-19	8-19		8-26	8-26	9-2	9-2	9-9	9-9	9-16	9-16	9-23	9-23	9-30	9-30
Australia																					
Sydney	8-10		8-14		8-21		8-28			9-4		9-11		9-18		9-25		10-2		10-9	
Melbourne	8-14		8-21		8-28		9-4			9-11		9-18		9-25		10-2		10-9		10-16	

Containership Service   Stacktrain Service   Truck Service

Red excites and makes us hungry. Yellow warns, and grabs for attention. Blue says integrity, dignity. Green, pastoral and reassuring, can invoke feelings of envy. Purple is royal; orange is hot.

Color is one of the most important design elements. It can be used to create a mood, attract attention, differentiate various sections of a publication, or tie multiple sections together. Think about what individual colors say, and assess how they work together when combined on a page.

Color methods

Designing and producing publications in color adds new levels of complexity to the page layout process. It must be approached with careful planning. Costs double or quadruple when two, four, or more pages of imagesetting, film, and plates for each printed page must be rerun because of a mistake. This makes proofreading, measurement, assignment of screen values, correct font identification, linking image files, and other production steps very important.

There are two methods for setting up a publication to print in color: spot color and process color. Spot color requires the use of a separate ink for each color you print. Process color uses four specified inks to produce the whole spectrum of color through a combination of screens. The method you use depends on several factors: your budget, the effect you wish to achieve, and the type of artwork the client provides.

Choosing colors

Swatch books are available from companies such as Pantone™, Trumatch, Focoltone and others, for both spot color and process color. For spot color, there are Pantone® books to show the hundreds of ink colors that can be created by mixing to a pre-set formula in the Pantone Matching System (PMS). These books come in small selector decks that fan out and have colors printed on both coated and uncoated papers. There are also specifier versions that have multiple chips of each color so they can be torn out and attached to mock-ups or paper samples to show clients or printers how the color will look.

Tint selectors show how various colors in screen levels—from 10% to 80%—look when printed; two color selectors show the result when two different colors are mixed; color and black selectors show the effect of black in combination with popular colors; and black colors and effects books show effects from the use of twelve different black tints.

For process color printing, the Trumatch Colorfinder books show hundreds of colors that can be created using combinations of percentages of the four process colors, cyan, magenta, yellow and black. (Page 40 to 43 of this book contains some formulas for creating colors based on CMYK.)

The Trumatch color selector.

The extravagant use of color in this annual
report ranges from duotone photos on the
left-hand page, to the vibrant illustration
on the right.
Designer: Dorothy A. Cross, Leimer Cross
Design, Seattle
Client: Nintendo Company, Ltd.

Accessing the submenu "Model" yields a selection of choices. These represent different color specification models for both spot and process color selection.

Color libraries in QuarkXPress

QuarkXPress's color handling begins with color libraries accessed through the Colors option under the Edit menu. As seen in the figure to the left, they include several spot and process color libraries. When you want to make a library available in Quark's color palette, choose the color you want from a swatch book (never use the screen display to judge color accuracy) and follow these steps:

1. Choose Colors from the Edit menu.

2. Click New, then select which color model you want to use, RGB, HSB, CMYK, Pantone©, Trumatch, or Focoltone. (Use CMYK for publications that will be commercially printed, and RGB for those that will be imaged to slides.)

3. After selecting the model decide whether or not the color should be set as process separations, if so this option should be selected.

4. Scroll through the list of available colors or type in the number if you know which one you are looking for. Selecting the color will define its name, however, you do have the option to change this if you so desire. Click OK.

5. Repeat the above steps until all of the colors have been defined, then save your selections to exit the color dialog box. The color's name will be added, in alphabetical order, to the color palette.

This represents the first dialog received after selecting the color option.

After you have selected a Pantone color to add to the Color palette you have the options of renaming the color or selecting it to Process seperate.

Spot Color

For the simplest color work—spot color—the printer mixes colored ink based on a formula. If you want a line of text and some boxes to be red, you supply the printer with numbers for the particular color of red you have chosen, two pieces of camera-ready art (one for black, one for red), and a tissue overlay or laser prints indicating which elements should print which color. You can use just one piece of camera-ready art if the two colors don't touch anywhere. When colors touch or one overprints another, two pieces of art (or separations) must be supplied. The printer prepares separate plates for the red and black inks.

Generally, use of more than three spot colors in a project is as expensive as full-color process printing. Unless there is a valid design reason—such as matching a company's logo colors perfectly, achieving vibrancy and intense clarity of color, or a requirement for special inks such as metallics or fluorescents —opt for process color when you require three or four different colors.

Designing with spot color

When using spot color, the guiding principle should be consistency. If one headline is in color, all headlines should be in the same color. Screened backgrounds in a color should not vary from one page to another without a specific reason for doing so.

Here are some design techniques that can be used with spot color:

- Use the second color for a graphic under the text.

- Use the second color for drop caps, headlines, lead-in text, or other styles.

- Create screened rectangles in a spot color for backgrounds.

- Use percentages of black ink in conjunction with the colored ink to make a third color.

- Print percentages in black ink under the colored ink to create additional shades of color.

Text in a spot color

When you want to print text in a second color, select the letters, words, or paragraphs with the Text tool. Click on your color choice in the color palette and the text will appear in the new color on screen. When you print the file, clicking Separations will give you the capability to choose separations if your print job requires them.

Graphic elements in a spot color

If your graphical elements are drawn in QuarkXPress, they will display the color attributes that you assign to them. If, however, they are imported from other programs, such as Aldus FreeHand, you will not see the QuarkXPress assigned color on screen. Note that if you are using a spot color (for example, Pantone 450) in QuarkXPress, and want to print an EPS graphic in that color, you can place a line drawing or grayscale drawing in EPS format that is black, and assign it the second color in the Color palette. Though the screen display will not show the graphic in color, it will print in the second color. If you want to print the graphic in black and the spot color, you must assign the colors in your graphics program.

The squares at the right, all of which are Pantone 450 in the color palette, have been assigned different percentage screen fills from the color palette.

Special spot colors

Spot colors that also add impact to any publication are fluorescents, pastels, and metallics. There are swatch books and specifiers for these colors that show the range of variations that you can achieve with these inks.

Two or more spot colors

Most often, a two-color publication features black for text, and a second color for graphics, rules, and other elements. It is not much more expensive to print with two colors instead of black and a color, and if chosen carefully, different screen percentages of two colors can be combined to yield a different third color.

Guidelines for spot color in QuarkXPress

It does not matter what colors appear on screen if you are using the spot color model for separation; simply ensure that items printing in the second color are identified as a color other than black. The color palette in default mode already lists Paper, Black, Registration, Blue, Red, Yellow, Magenta, Cyan and Green as color choices. In order to assign a color to an element, you must have that element selected and the color palette open. Although it is possible to set up a publication specifying the actual number(s) of the Pantone or other color model, it is not necessary to do so if you are using spot rather than process color separation. You can use any of QuarkXPress's default colors (Red, Blue, Green) to specify color items. This is particularly useful if you have not made a final decision about which spot color you want to use. Rather than specifying PMS 547 for the blue your client has not yet approved, use the default Blue to select all the items that appear in blue. This way, if and when your client chooses a different color of blue at the last minute, you won't run the risk of having a wrong PMS number output on the bottom of the high-resolution film. That would cause confusion for the printer.

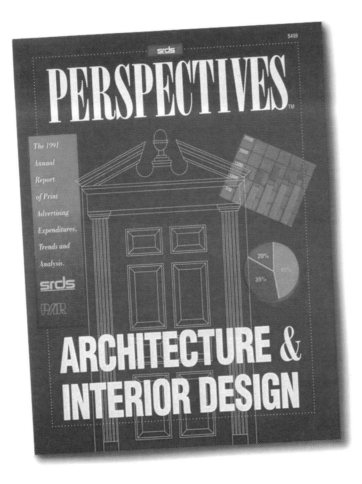

The cover at the left shows the use of two spot colors, blue and magenta. When mixed, they form a range of purple colors.
Designer: Beth Bast, Beth Bast Designs, Chicago
Client: SRDS

Process color

Process color is the printing of any color or range of colors by mixing them from a combination of different levels of four basic process inks: cyan, magenta, yellow, and black (CMYK). A color separation is a breakdown of a full-color photograph or other art into four process color components, performed by electronic or mechanical means. Metal or paper printing plates are made from each of these four elements, and as they are printed in registration, one after another, they result in a full-color approximation of the original photo or illustration.

QuarkXPress can perform process color separations when outputting final pages on a high-resolution imagesetter—or on a laser printer for proofing purposes. If you have scanned or drawn color graphics in your document, the program breaks those graphics down into their cyan, magenta, yellow and black components when you choose Separations in the Print dialog box (see below).

Designing with process color

Using process color increases the complexity of your project by geometric proportions. There is so much to know about color printing, and so much that can go wrong if you make a mistake, that it may be better to supply your printer with the color photographs or graphics you want to use, and have them stripped in conventionally. Still, there are times when that is an extra challenge because you are using color backgrounds, color type, or other techniques.

When using four-color process printing, the tremendous choice of colors gives you many design options. Part of the challenge at hand is to narrow down those options.

■ Get a Trumatch book or other process color selector and pick out a range of a few colors to serve as your basic palette. Or, you can choose color formulas from the following pages.

■ If you have a Pantone spot color selector, you can choose the colors from that library in QuarkXPress, but they will be CMYK equivalents when separated—not as vibrant and not true to the color chips in the book.

■ You can create backgrounds, just as you can with spot color. Assigning different screen values to them will make them lighter or darker.

■ With QuarkXPress you also have the option to select gradient backgrounds in different colors. It is possible to gradate from a pantone (CMYK equivalent) to another color such as black. Below is a possible example when using this option.

Text in process color

You can assign any color you wish to text in process color, but it is not a good idea for small point sizes. This is because printing plates or paper may shift in commercial printing—especially true on a web press—and one or more colors may print out of register. This can yield red type with a yellow "halo"—hard to read and messy looking.

Graphic elements in process color

If you are using process color, try to avoid very thin rules—for the same reason as small point sizes of type—misregistration in printing may cause blurring.

Imported scans of color photographs or illustrations are broken down automatically into their CMYK components when you use QuarkXPress for separation.

	C	M	Y	K
	0	9	4	0
	0	8	10	0
	0	2	7	0
	4	0	9	0
	10	0	9	6

	C	M	Y	K
	0	25	21	6
	0	22	40	24
	0	2	40	6
	22	0	50	0
	34	0	40	0

	C	M	Y	K
	6	55	55	6
	0	45	55	0
	0	8	36	0
	16	0	36	20
	70	0	60	24

0	0	0
70	85	100
58	85	90
17	15	30
0	0	0
39	65	65
70	75	100
24	0	18
0	5	0
0	0	21
70	85	100
0	0	0
13	13	28
0	0	0
70	70	100
0	24	52
100	100	100
0	0	0
98	100	100
27	0	72

	C	M	Y	K
	9	0	2	0
	36	0	8	6
	50	0	28	0
	10	4	0	0
	36	8	0	0
	55	39	0	24
	3	10	0	0
	0	40	0	18
	23	41	0	0
	7	9	10	0
	16	13	21	6
	36	50	55	24
	4	0	2	8
	7	4	0	18
	0	8	3	24

	C	M	Y	K
	77	0	17	6
	100	0	0	30
	4	82	16	0
	65	90	100	0
	4	0	9	30

	C	M	Y	K
	80	0	25	30
	85	76	0	6
	42	75	0	0
	55	77	85	24
	8	2	10	42

	C	M	Y	K
	77	0	17	42
	100	70	0	24
	0	100	0	42
	45	60	100	6
	0	10	9	42

Using color libraries with process color

You can choose from any or all of the color libraries if you are printing in process color. Make rules, screens, and other graphics any color you can find or create under the Colors command. If you fill a box with a Trumatch blue-green with a specific number, when you go to final output, the program can separate that fill, break it down into percentages of cyan, magenta, yellow and black that when combined will closely match the color you selected from the book.

Automatic color separation

Even though QuarkXPress will color separate full color photographs, consider printing some photos as color monotones to achieve a more graphic effect. This can be done as follows:

1. If your scan is full-color, either rescan the image as grayscale and save in TIFF format, or reopen it in an image processing program such as Adobe Photoshop and convert it to grayscale.

2. Place the scan into QuarkXPress with the Get Picture command under the File menu.

3. With the image selected, choose a color from the color palette.

4. When color separation takes place, the image appears to be a monotone (various levels of one color), even though the one color it is made up of will be composed of different amounts of Cyan, Magenta, Yellow, and Black.

The Color Palette

You can find the color palette under the View menu. A description of each element of the color palette follows:

■ **Palette menu**

A color selection can be made to include both the fill and surrounding line of an element, the fill only, or the line only. Clicking on either the square icon or the line icon selects an object's fill or its line, if you have selected the object.

■ **Black**

[Black] must be assigned to text or other elements with care. Like other QuarkXPress colors, Black knocks out by default. The difference is that text colored 100% Black overprints by default. You cannot edit the default Black, so if you want a black that overprints objects, follow this procedure:

1. Choose Colors from the Edit menu.

2. Click New.

3. Choose CMYK Model.

4. Select the base color [Black].

6. Make sure tint is set at 100%.

7. Name your new black "Black 2" or something similar to distinguish it from default [Black];

8. Select the trap information option and select it to overprint.

9. Click OK.

If you do this, make sure any black elements you wish to overprint are changed from the default black to your new black.

■ **Registration**

Choose the Registration option when an item must print on all separations. For instance, crop marks that you have drawn yourself, registration marks, or job identification information such as file names, creator names, etc. This option should not be confused with QuarkXPress's printer marks, also known as Registration marks.

■ **Blue, Green and Red**

Blue, Green and Red are default colors in the program, and if you have chosen specific colors from a library, you may want to remove these. This is easy to accomplish following this procedure:

1. Choose Colors from the Edit menu.

2. Select Red, Blue or Green.

3. Click on Delete.

4. Click on the Save button.

If you attempt to remove a color and have previously assigned an element that color, QuarkXPress will ask if you want to change all elements in that color to [Black]. Black, Registration, Cyan, Magenta, and Yellow are colors that cannot be removed from the color palette.

Four-color black

There is black—and there is really black. When using four-color process printing, you may want to add a four-color black. Four-color black has a depth that cannot be found simply by printing one pass of black ink. Instead, it combines all four colors at various percentages. You can see in the example below how four-color black is different from plain black. (Never use four-color black for type because it creates registration problems. But for backgrounds and other graphics, it works very well.) Here is how to make it:

1. Choose Colors from the Edit menu.

2. Select New.

3. Choose CMYK; type in the name 4-color black to distinguish it from regular black, and select 100% for black, and 60% for Cyan, Magenta and Yellow.

4. Click on the Save button.

black

four-color black

Combining process and spot color

If you have a large printing budget, you may want to use more than four colors. It is not unusual to specify five or even six colors—for example, CMYK, a Pantone color, and a spot varnish. Any more than six colors will require a specialized printing press.

When you use a fifth color, it can be applied as a premixed ink, or as a CMYK combination. QuarkXPress enables you to designate whether individual colors should be treated as process, or spot, when outputting the files. Confusion may occur when you use Pantone or other color library formulas in a document printed in process color. The color libraries may contain formulas for color separation to CMYK for objects designated by a Colorcurve, DaiNippon, Pantone, or Toyo spot color. Spot colors are broken down into their process equivalents. The process equivalents of pre-mixed ink colors are rarely exact matches. If you want to make a strong impact with a particular color, consider printing it as a fifth, spot color.

Color effects

There are two easy ways to add color to any publication, even if you are only printing in black.

One of the least expensive methods is to print on colored paper. Combining different colors for separate pages can be effective if the colors are complementary. Call paper suppliers in your region and ask them for sample books, or sample sheets of a particular paper you have in mind. Find out whether the paper is in stock or if it requires special ordering. Usually only the largest print runs justify the quantities required by suppliers for a special order.

Another way to get a sense of color into a publication being printed in black only, is to think of white, black, and the levels of grays as colors. With its screening capabilities, QuarkXPress can provide a wide array of gray choices for any page. Using the range of grays effectively is a challenge for any designer, and can result in distinctive and handsome documents. Don't be heavy-handed. Seek subtlety and rhythm, balance, and contrast in your use of grays and they will add color to your pages.

There are the various screen values found either in the color palette or under the Item menu under Modify. You can make any text or object print in a much wider range of gray levels by creating your own gray colors. Follow these steps:

1. Choose Colors from the Edit menu.

2. Select New to create an additional color.

3. Choose the CMYK model and set the Black level to any percentage between 1% and 99%. (Note: it is difficult for many printing processes to hold screens below 10%, or for any screen values higher than 90% to be distinguishable from black.)

4. Name your new color, (e.g., 25% black) and click on the OK button. The name is added in alphabetical order to the color palette as choice, and you can select that color for type or graphics.

5. Click Save to exit the Color dialog box.

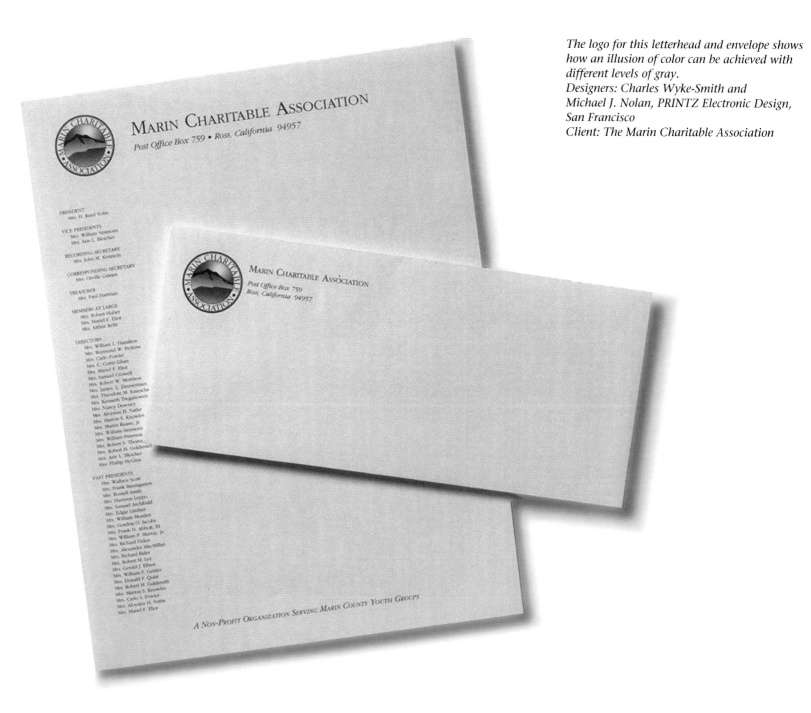

The logo for this letterhead and envelope shows how an illusion of color can be achieved with different levels of gray.
Designers: Charles Wyke-Smith and Michael J. Nolan, PRINTZ Electronic Design, San Francisco
Client: The Marin Charitable Association

Overprinting

The questions posed by overprinting can be confusing for many people. When using two colors, the darker color is generally printed after the lighter one. This means that black text appearing on a yellow box will be printed on top of the box. If you are printing blue text on a yellow box, you could get a color mix of green text. To avoid this mix, you can make sure the text knocks out of the box below it. That means the camera-ready art for the yellow layer will show the type reversed out. To further complicate matters, items that don't overprint generally need to be trapped. (See Trapping, page 49.)

In QuarkXPress, all colors are set to have an absolute trap of 0.144 with an overprint limit of 95%. You can specify that individual QuarkXPress-drawn elements overprint. For example, if you want a red circle to knock out of the black box that surrounds it, by using the Trap Information dialog box you can select the circle and tell it to knock out. The Trap Information dialog box can be found by selecting the View menu and choosing the Show Trap information option then releasing the mouse.

If you want certain attributes of a QuarkXPress-drawn object to overprint, here is how it works. Note that in this example the circle has a 1 point black border which is being changed to overprint.

1. Select the object with the Pointer tool.

2. Choose the Show Trap info dialog box from the View menu.

3. Indicate if you want the inside or outside to print over the object(s) placed behind it. If you do not choose Overprint, the fill or line will use the default trap of 0.144.

If you wish to make a color—and all objects assigned to that color—overprint rather than knock out, here is how to do it:

1. Choose Colors from the Edit menu.

2. Select the existing color you wish to use for overprinting.

3. Click Edit Trap. Click the Overprint option for all of the colors in the palette. Click OK. Click Save to exit the Color palette.

If you want some objects in a color to overprint, and other objects in the same color to knock out, here's how that's done:

1. Choose Colors from the Edit menu.

2. Click New.

3. Type the name of the new color that distinguishes it as the knock out color (Blue K/O).

4. Choose the base color.

6. Set the trap to Automatic.

7. Click OK and then Save to exit the Colors dialog box.

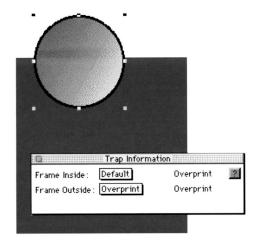

Trapping

Trapping is a production issue that may cause confusion. While the concept is simple to understand, it can be difficult to achieve consistent results. Trapping is the overlapping of separate colors to prevent gaps during the printing process. Trapping is one of those printer's arts, developed and refined over decades, that only recently has fallen into the lap of the designer through the power of electronic publishing. For that reason, it makes more sense to leave trapping to the experts—commercial printers—rather than attempt it yourself.

Trapping is necessary because different colors of ink are not laid down at the same time on the printing press. They are printed in succession. While a good commercial printer makes every attempt to keep all plates in registration, many factors—such as paper expansion or shrinkage, temperature, ink coverage, and so forth—may cause misregistration. When that happens, one color prints out of alignment with the others, and gaps may appear where the colors were supposed to meet. To prevent gaps, trapping was developed to slightly overlap colors where they touch.

These pages present only a brief overview of trapping so that you can understand its implications. You should talk to your commercial printer about trapping before you get too far into the development of your project. It is also important to talk to your service bureau and get advice as well.

Here is some information about trapping you should know:

- Trapping is generally most important with spot color jobs where the different colors overlap each other.

- Trapping is more an issue if you are having your job printed on a high-speed web press, less so on a sheet-fed press.

- There are two terms used commonly for traps: spread and choke. Spread means that a stroke is added to an inner, lighter color. Choke is when a stroke is added to the inner edge of a surrounding, lighter color.

- Your commercial printer often can compensate for potential trapping problems by exposing film slightly longer when making plates. This process subtly increases the width of lines. Don't just assume that this will be the case; talk to the printer.

- Your service bureau may be able to perform excellent trapping using additional software such as Aldus TrapWise rather than you performing the trapping.

Page layout

QuarkXPress is a page layout program that covers a number of functions. This section discusses basic page considerations, such as what size paper you use, the use of master pages, setting up a grid, automatic page numbering, sorting page order, setting up pages for bleeds, and so forth.

The size of the page below is indicated by the pair of shoes at the bottom of it. QuarkXPress can be used to create pages that will print this large or larger; it's just a matter of planning. Designer: Ron Louie, Pentagram Design, New York
Client: Cactus

Page sizes

If the publication is something the reader can display, such as a poster or calendar, an oversize page may be necessary. If you want the reader to file the document for further reference, it is important that it fit into a file folder. If you are designing a card or invitation, be certain there are envelopes already made to size that it will fit into snugly. If it is to be kept in a pocket or wallet, it must be small enough to do so.

Choose a page size that allows printing on standard sizes of paper and printing presses—or be prepared to pay a premium.

Standard paper sizes

Odd page sizes can mean waste and extra cost. Before you choose a page size, determine what size sheet your job will be printed on. Also determine how to best utilize the sheet to eliminate the amount lost to trimming. Consult your printer on this matter because various printing presses use different sizes of paper.

- 8 $^1/_2$" x 11"
- 11" x 17"
- 23" x 35"
- 24" x 36"
- 25" x 35"
- 25" x 38"
- 35" x 45"
- 38" x 50"

Standard page trims

There are some standard trimmed page sizes that correspond to the sizes paper comes in. For instance, 24 individual sheets of 4" x 9" can be cut from a single sheet of 24" x 36" paper. Some of the most common are:

- 4" x 9"
- 4 $^1/_4$" x 5 $^3/_8$"
- 4 $^1/_2$" x 6"
- 5 $^1/_2$" x 8 $^1/_2$"
- 6" x 9"
- 8 $^1/_2$" x 11"
- 9" x 12"

Standard envelopes

It is expensive to have envelopes custom-made—and also just the kind of time-consuming work that may throw an entire project off schedule if the need comes as a surprise at the last minute. Therefore, it is usually best to design with standard sizes and types of envelopes in mind. Some of the standard sizes (and their shorthand names) are as follows:

- No. 6   3 $^3/_8$" x 6"
- No. 10   4 $^1/_8$" x 9 $^1/_2$"
- No. 9 $^1/_2$"
  (Booklet)   9" x 12"
- No. 13   10" x 13"
- A-2   4 $^3/_8$" x 5 $^5/_8$"
- A-6   4 $^3/_4$" x 6 $^1/_2$"
- A-7   5 $^1/_4$" x 7 $^1/_4$"
- A-8   5 $^1/_2$" x 8 $^1/_8$"
- A-10   6 $^1/_4$" x 9 $^5/_8$"

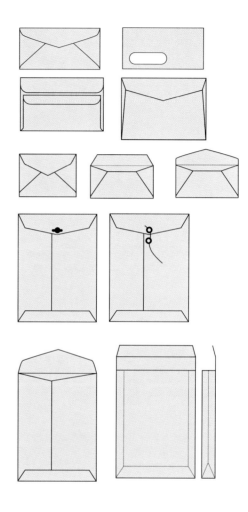

The diagram above shows different envelope types, from commercial on the top left to window, announcement, catalog, booklet, and expandable styles.

51

Page sizes that get attention

Sometimes, page size is dictated by the need to grab attention. If that is the case, consider a very small or very large page. Shapes can grab attention, too. A square page makes an unusual statement and is quite easy to work with. A diagonal trim prior to folding can add variation to an invitation or brochure.

Non-standard page sizes

For projects such as a letterhead or business cards, it is necessary to adhere to standards. Business cards should always be 2" by 3 1/2" because many people who receive them file them in standard card holders or other files. (This does not mean that they cannot have clever flaps, folds, die cuts, or other creative devices.) Letterhead must fit into typewriters, printers, or envelopes and should always be 8 1/2" X 11".

Folding options

Folding by a printer requires prior planning. Although the printer usually performs the task by machine, you should hand-fold sample sheets of the paper the publication will be printed on. This gives you a feel for the folding characteristics. For instance, does one side look different than the other? Is the grain going in the wrong direction? Does it need to be scored by the printer before it is folded? Talk to your printer about the folding and make sure it is included in the bid.

There are many ways to fold paper. The folds are an integral part of the design. Plan for, and around, folds and make the most of them. They can be treated as an invisible element, or they can be used to define sections or pages. Unique folds can be part of the "hook" of any publication. Here is some information you need to know about folding:

- There are two basic kinds of folds, parallel and right angle. It is also possible to fold at an angle, but this is difficult and requires handwork by the printer.

- If you are using a heavy paper stock, it probably will need to be scored before it is folded. Pay particular attention to scoring if your paper stock is coated, a foil, a duplex, or other specialty.

- Trimming, scoring, perforating, pasting, and slitting can all be done with attachments to a folding machine.

- Panels can be created through different types of parallel and right angle folds: four, six, eight, twelve, and sixteen pages.

This striking self-promotion piece for a design firm makes the most of both unusual page size and folding.
Design: Bay Graphics, Berkeley, CA

A quick measurement for folds

If you are setting up a number of folds on a large page, you can quickly measure where the fold lines should be—even if you have complicated margins:

1. Temporarily change the document setup so that the margin measurement is zero in all categories. (You may want to jot down the margin specifications if they are complex, because you will need to reenter them later.)

2. Go to the master guides under the Page menu and change column guides to the number of folds you wish to use. Specify 0 for column width.

3. Draw ruler guides out to the column markers from the Ruler.

4. Change Page Setup back to the original specifications. Now viewing any page reflects both the new margins and accurate, pre-measured fold lines.

Indicating fold lines

If you are using a common fold (such as fold in thirds), it is usually not necessary for you to indicate on the final artwork where the fold lines should be. However, if you are going to trim your page, or you intend to have uneven folds, or overlapping folds, you must indicate where they should be. Fold marks are very easy to make with QuarkXPress using the following steps:

1. Make sure you are on the master page.

2. Drag a ruler guide to where you want the fold.

3. Choose the line tool and specify a dotted line from the measurements palette.

4. Select Registration from the color palette. Lines then will appear on the artwork for all colors when separated.

5. Draw a dotted line that just touches the edge of the page and extends $1/4$" beyond the edge. The line prints in final imagesetting, but will not interfere with artwork that bleeds. (If it does interfere, the printer probably can mask it out later.)

6. Step and repeat this line by setting both the horizontal and vertical offset to 0 (zero). Holding down the Shift key, drag the pasted line to the other edge of the page.

7. Step and repeat both lines; Shift-drag them to the next fold.

Indicating crop lines

If you want an unusual trim—such as an angle, you must indicate the crop marks manually, rather than using QuarkXPress's automatic crop marks feature.

1. On the master page, use horizontal and vertical ruler guides to define the four sides of your trimmed page.

2. Choose a .5 pt solid line and Registration from the color palette.

3. $1/4$" to the left of the left-hand vertical ruler guide, draw a $1/2$" horizontal line along the top measurement. Step and repeat the lines and shift-drag the pasted line to the bottom horizontal measurement.

4. Step and repeat both lines, and shift drag them until they are $1/4$" to the right of the right-hand vertical measurement line.

5. Repeat the process for vertical trim lines.

Master pages

Master pages should be the first pages you work on when you open a new document. They are where you build your grid, set automatic page numbering, create common headers and footers, folding marks, and similar elements that will repeat through-out the document.

Items placed on master pages may be displayed on the individual pages of your document.

You can change guidelines on individual pages as well as any of the other elements without affecting the master pages. This is one of the unique features which Quark has over other page layout applications.

Establishing the grid

The grid is an invisible division of the page into equal, measured parts. Think of a grid as you would the ironwork for a tall building—necessary to ensure a beautiful structure. Of course, the grid can be broken when you choose to do so, but unless it is there to begin with, you cannot achieve the necessary balance, rhythm, and organization in your publication. Decide whether you want a perfectly balanced page or a more dynamic one with an off-center approach.

Establishing margins

The first principle in establishing margins is to make the bottom margin larger than the sides or top, as you usually see in framed pictures. (This looks best because the optical center of a page is actually higher than the exact center.)

Treat white space as an active element in your page design. Whether it serves the function of a place to rest the thumbs when holding the book open, or a place to rest the eyes when viewing an ad, white space is essential, and should be treated as such.

As with all rules, those about margins and white space can be broken—as long as they are first understood.

Establishing columns

Columns are basic design elements that you can use to increase readability and organize information. Columns have great aesthetic impact on any document, and should be used consistently from page to page. Columns should be separated by the correct amount of white space—too much or too little can make them look awkward. You may need to experiment with column widths and spacing before you get it right.

- If you are using a small point size, you should use narrower columns; a large point size dictates a wider column for better readability.

- Set columns on the master pages.

- Columns of equal width are not always the right design solution; for instance, a three-column page with a narrow outside column and two wider inside columns can be very versatile. Setting columns this way cannot be done automatically, however. You must set three equal columns and then adjust them manually.

- Occasionally, a specific part of a page can contain different numbers of columns. This kind of arrangement still should be based on a grid, otherwise it can look haphazard and confusing.

This fold-out map was designed for a museum exhibit. Notice how it makes use of different column widths: six on the top half of the page, and twelve on the bottom. Also note how photos and accompanying captions are balanced between columns—an effective way to break the monotony that repetitiveness might produce.
Designer: Christina Freyss, Pentagram Design, New York
Client: Cooper-Hewitt Museum

Inposition

This function, another QuarkXPress XTension by DK&A, enables the designer of a publication to perform what is called "imposition," or structuring pages in the proper order and relationship to one another for printing back to back. It creates a copy of your publication with the pages arranged in the proper printing order. Imposition is a function that was performed traditionally by prepress professionals, and it refers to the arrangement of pages for multi-page spreads or signatures. While it can be instructive to perform this function yourself, it is a task best left to an expert—your printer. There are so many variables to consider: bleeds, graphics printed across two pages, registration marks, etc., that it is risky to try and impose anything but the simplest booklet yourself. If you want to do your own imposition with build booklet, use the XTension only when your publication is completely finished. Here is how it works:

1. Choose INposition from the Utilities menu.

2. Select whether you want to build the booklet by first and last pages, or by the signature method of groups of 16 pages.

3. INposition will create a new, untitled file with the pages in the proper order; close your original QuarkXPress file. Name and save the new file.

Automatic page numbering

QuarkXPress offers a variety of ways to number your pages. You have a choice of three options: page number of previous text box, page number of current text box, and page number of next text box.

Command+3 is the keyboard command for setting automatic page numbering for the current text box. If placed on the master pages, the page numbers will appear on every page throughout the document. (This can be done on individual pages and the pages will display their correct number, if you are numbering only certain ones.) Here is how automatic page numbering works:

1. Create a text box in the correct place on the page by selecting the Text tool. Click down on the mouse button, drag the mouse and release the button before you begin typing.

2. Type Command+3. If done correctly you should see something like <#>.

3. After inserting the first automatic page number, select its text box and set the proper type specifications for font, size, style, and alignment. You also can make modifications such as typing "Page" in front of the number marker, etc.

4. Use the Pointer tool to ensure you have anchored the handles of the text box on the correct margins or columns.

Sorting page order

Often it becomes necessary to change the order in which pages appear. If you are using automatic page numbering, it is extremely important that the correct page order be established and maintained.

When you have the need to change the order of pages, you simply use the Document Layout palette rearrange representations of your actual pages. QuarkXPress automatically re-arranges and re-numbers your pages.

In this example page 9 is being moved to become page 5, thus causing all of the pages after that point to shift by one page.

Bleeds

A bleed is a graphic, screen, or text that extends up to the edge of the page trim. Because printing presses require a gripping edge on the paper as it is fed, ink extending all the way to the edge of the sheet will be picked up by the rollers and smeared. If you use a bleed, paper larger than the finished publication must be used, and then trimed after the pages are dry. This generally means the printer will charge more.

Bleeds are one of the designer's most effective tools for photographs, solid colors, screens, or backgrounds. They create a sense that there is more to be seen, as if the idea being depicted is too big to be contained on a simple page.

If you intend to use a bleed, before you choose a size for your printed piece, make sure that there is a standard sheet size that will allow for the trimming. (For a list of sheet sizes, see page 51.)

When setting up the bleed in QuarkXPress, simply position or resize the artwork, screen, or solid color $\frac{1}{4}$" off the edge of the page on all sides where you want the bleed. Remember that laser printers do not print an image to the edge of the paper, so you won't see the bleed on a laser proof. High-resolution imagesetters print outside the defined page, enabling you to set up the artwork properly.

For proofing purposes, to show how the bleed will look on laser prints, reduce the percentage of the page and specify crop marks when you print. Then use a straight edge and blade to trim at the crop marks. Or, manually tile the page, specify crop marks, trim the excess, paste up the tiles by hand and trim the edges.

When using bleeds on an envelope, be aware that the printing will be done on flat sheets that will be converted to envelopes after they are printed. This will add time to a project and increase the cost. Know how long it will take to do the conversion and what the printer will charge for doing it before designing a bleed on an envelope.

To set up bleeds like those in the Blue Sky Design corporate identity package, follow these guidelines:

1. Set the zero point to the top right-hand corner of your page by clicking in the box where the rulers intersect and dragging to the corner of the page.

2. Ensure that any element measures at least $\frac{1}{4}$" outside on each side where it is to bleed. In the case of the blue sky—which in the actual design is a scanned photo—it must exceed the boundary of the page on the top and on the left-hand side.

3. When setting up bleeds on a document with double-sided facing pages, such as a book or brochure, remember that bleeds can be created only for the top, bottom and outside edges. To get the appearance of a bleed on an inside edge, bring your image or color exactly to the edge of the page.

58

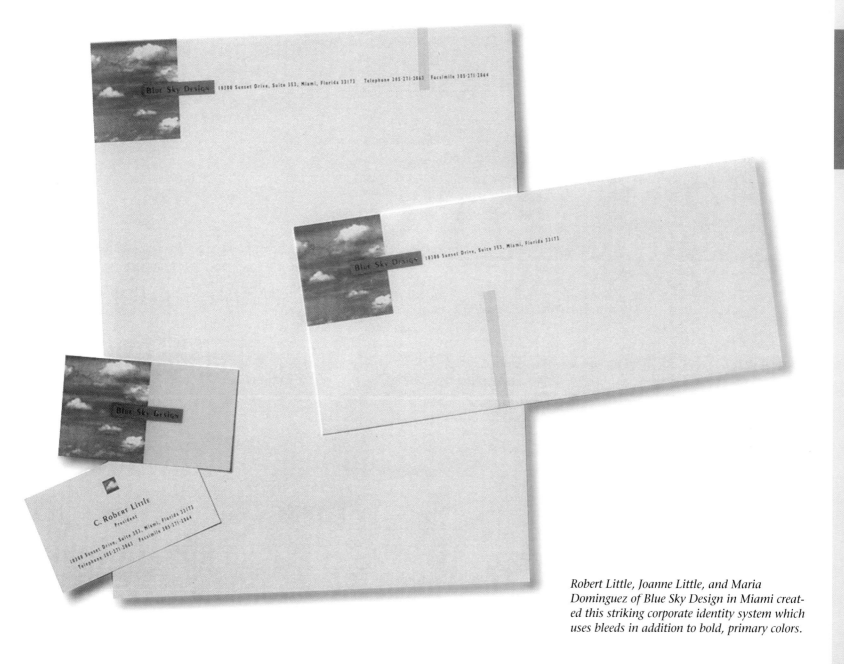

Robert Little, Joanne Little, and Maria Dominguez of Blue Sky Design in Miami created this striking corporate identity system which uses bleeds in addition to bold, primary colors.

Measurement

Precise measurement is one of the most valuable capabilities of QuarkXPress. Even the most compulsive designer can be satisfied by the accuracy of the program. With 400% magnification, moveable zero points, Snap to Guides, vertical and horizontal rules, Measurement palettes, and the other measuring capabilities, you won't need rulers and T-squares.

Preferences

A study of QuarkXPress's measurement tools should begin with the Preferences under the Edit menu. Here is where you determine which measurement system to use. This menu enables you to choose whether you display guidelines in front or in back of text and graphics.

Under Edit menu preferences you can access functions that were designed to enable you to tailor the program to the style in which you most like to work.

- QuarkXPress's Measurement system gives you the option to measure in inches, decimal inches, picas, millimeters, or ciceros. While each of these measurement systems has its place, most graphic artists prefer to measure in picas, partly because the measurement system is compatible with the measurement of point sizes. Some designers use inches for a measurement system, and picas for the vertical ruler.

- This is where you decide whether guidelines are in front of or behind the graphics and text on the page. You can change how the guides are displayed if you have trouble grabbing them for movement.

- Horizontal and Vertical nudge distances can be changed here in greater or lesser increments for use with the Measurements palette.

- Graying out detailed graphics, greek pictures, will speed up the performance when you are doing things to the file that do not require viewing graphics in detail.

Rulers

Rulers are another very useful feature of QuarkXPress and work with flawless simplicity.

- If rulers are not visible, you can display them by choosing Show Rulers from the View menu.

- By moving the Pointer over the horizontal ruler, you can click and drag out non-printing horizontal ruler guides and check their position with the dotted lines indicated on the vertical ruler. The same is true for vertical ruler guides whose position is indicated on the horizontal ruler.

- When you first open a publication, the zero measurements on the rulers are at the top, left-hand edge of the page. You can change this by clicking in the corner where the horizontal and vertical rulers intersect and dragging out the dotted lines. Where you release the mouse button is where you will find the new zero point measurement. This is useful for measuring specific distances between elements.

Guides

Guides are the backbone of QuarkXPress's measurement system. Here are some of their features:

- They can be turned on or off by choosing Show Guides from the View menu. Turning them off makes a visible difference when evaluating the aesthetics of a layout.

- You can use the Snap to guides feature under the View menu to easily align items to the guides.

- Common guides for all pages should be set on the master pages. Once you are on individual pages those guides can be moved.

Magnification

The ability to see a magnified view of your page is very helpful when working on a small monitor, or whenever you want to see text or graphics up close.

- The View menu under Layout will allow you to change the display from Fit in window to 200% size. You can use the commands listed, or drag and release on the size you want.

- A useful method for changing the view is to hold the Option and Command key while you click the mouse. This will toggle between 100% and 200% views.

- Another option is to manually type in the percentage you desire in the lower left corner of the active screen.

- The magnification tool can be predefined to zoom in at percentages that you define. This can be done by modifying the magnification tool under the Preferences option within the Edit menu.

Measurements palette

The Measurements palette is another way for a user to make very precise measurements. With this tool, you can manipulate text or objects with great precision by entering exact values for placement. The Measurements palette also enables you to make several kinds of alterations without switching to another menu or choosing commands.

- Access the Measurements palette by choosing it under the View menu. It can be moved to more convenient locations on your page by using the Pointer tool, clicking on the left-hand side bar and dragging.

- Measurements palette options change depending on what object is selected. Also, if you select more than one item, the control palette options will be limited to those functions that can be performed on all objects at once.

The red rectangle is selected, and the Measurements palette gives its location on the X & Y axis, its height and width as originally drawn, and its angle of rotation (0°).

When the X axis is changed from 0.91" to 2.698" and the enter key is pressed, the red triangle moves to the right.

Now the value width for the red triangle is changed from 2.014" to 3.514". As the Enter key is pressed, the rectangle takes on the new dimensions.

- The reference point proxy enables you to define which point on the object that you are transforming will be the base point for a measurement, move, rotation, skew, or reflection. You simply click on the handle in the proxy that you want to use as the reference point. In the examples here, the reference point is the center of the object.

- To execute your transformation, once you have selected the proper measurements, press the return key.

- You may even use arthmetic in the numeric fields To make a 1" box $1/2$" wider enter +.5 after the 1 inch width and press the return key.

The red rectangle is selected, and rotated 45°.

The red rectangles is selected and has its height changed.

Formatting text with the Measurements palette

The measurements palette enables you to format text when using the text tool. You can hide or display the Measurements palette by selecting it from the View menu.

- You can apply character attributes that you would normally find under the Type menu (Command+Shift+D), such as font, size, leading, etc., to the text you have selected.

- You can also select alignment, styles, and other paragraph options that you would normally find under the Formats submenu (Command+Shift+F) to text in which you have placed the cursor.

- After selecting or clicking a text option on the Measurement palette, the attributes are applied to the selected text immediately. If you type a value for an option, you must apply the new setting by pressing Tab or Return.

Sizing

The Pointer tool enables you to size graphics or text blocks. Using the Point tool, click on the text or graphic block to select it, point at one of the handles, and drag the mouse to make the graphic or text block larger or smaller. Holding down the Shift+Command+Option keys when resizing imported graphics will keep them proportional.

Holding down the Shift key when resizing QuarkXPress-drawn objects will cause them to reshape to a square or a circle, depending on whether the Rectangle or Ellipse tool was used to draw them.

Here are some shortcuts that you can use when sizing:

■ If you have aligned your text block to the top guideline, use the bottom handles of the text block to narrow or widen the text block. This way, the vertical alignment of the text block will be unaffected.

■ If one side of a graphic is properly aligned, use the opposite handle for resizing—resulting in less additional measurement.

Rotation

QuarkXPress has the ability to rotate text and graphics at any angle. Following these steps it is easy to use:

1. Select the text block or graphic with the Pointer tool.

2. Change to the Rotating tool in the Toolbox and position the cursor at a fixed point. (The location around which you want to rotate the object.)

3. Click and drag the cursor away from the fixed point in the direction you want to rotate the object. You will obtain more control if you drag the cursor a longer distance away, just as you would with a lever.

4. Release the mouse button when the object is in position.

5. To restrain the rotation in 45° increments, hold the Shift key down as you rotate.

After you have rotated the text, you can edit it without undoing the rotation. Simply select the text or insert the cursor with the Text tool and make the edits.

Skewing or reflecting objects

By using the Measurements palette, it is possible to skew or reflect text or graphics.

1. Select the text block or graphic with the Pointer tool.

2. Open the Measurements palette by choosing it under the View menu.

3. To skew, choose a reference point from which to skew, and change the skewing value. Click the Apply button.

4. To reflect, choose a reference point from which to reflect, and click either the Horizontal-reflecting button or the Vertical-reflecting button.

Most publications are mailed and the designer must be aware of how the piece will be packaged (and how it will hold up in the mail) before initial design begins. If you are doing anything out of the ordinary, begin your design research at the post office. Ask about sizes, weights, closures, rates, and any other factors that will influence how and what you design.

Envelopes

If you intend to mail your publication in an envelope, check that there is a standard-size in a matching or coordinating paper, and that the printed piece fits well in the envelope. Don't ruin the impact of a beautifully produced publication with an envelope that's a hasty, cheap afterthought—too large (or worse, too small) for the publication inside. (See page 51 for standard envelope sizes.)

Self-mailers

If the publication is a self-mailer, consider where the name and address will go, how much postage will be required based on weight of the paper and the number of pages, and how the printed piece will hold up through handling by the post office. You may want to design a wrapper for your publication that is saddle-stitched (stapled) to it. A wrapper can be made of heavy cover stock, semi-transparent stock, or other contrasting paper and designed to be discarded, or kept as part of the piece.

Newsletters are often self-mailers. If you are creating a four-page newsletter that measures 8 $\frac{1}{2}$" x 11" before it is folded, you have the option of folding it in half or thirds for mailing. This has implications for the design:

■ Don't allow headlines or photographs to be cut by folds.

■ Place an interesting article on the top section of the back page. Repeat your masthead as a smaller version on the back page to immediately identify the publication.

■ Determine how to close the pages for mailing. Sealing wax, string, seals and stickers, staples, or other closing devices have an impact on your design.

The newsletter to the left illustrates a reduced version of a nameplate from the front page for mailing purposes on the back page.
Designer: Michael J. Nolan
Client: Suzanne Clark Productions, San Francisco

Postage PAID marks

Postage marks look best if they are the same size and proportions as a normal (rather than special issue) postage stamp. Use the following steps to make them:

1. Choose the Measurements palette from the View menu.

2. Select the Text tool from the Toolbox and draw a small rectangle.

3. Bring the Width and Height measurements on the Control palette to .9" x 1.2" as you draw the rectangle, or adjust the rectangle to those measurements after it is drawn.

4. Add a .5 black line to the drawn rectangle.

5. Center the cursor by typing Command-C before you enter the following information: U.S. (Return) POSTAGE (Return) P A I D (Return) Permit No. (Return) XXXXXXXX (for number).

6. Change the text to a sans serif face such as Helvetica, Futura, or Avant Garde.

7. Double-click on each line and adjust the point sizes until they fit inside the rectangle. The letters should not touch the outside lines, and PAID should be much larger and bolder than the other words.

8. Change the leading method to have a Baseline Shift of -5 points or select the text box to have a 6 point text inset. This can be done by selecting the Modify option under the menu or by pressing Command+m.

Reduced nameplates

Rather than simply typing the name of the organization sponsoring the publication, if it has a nameplate, copy and reduce that element as the identifier on the mailing page. This lends consistency and professionalism to a document. The mailing page is also a good place for the publication's masthead: who publishes it, the address, the board of directors, and similar information.

U.S.
POSTAGE
PAID
Permit No.
456789

Don't overlook QuarkXPress's usefulness for making signs. Your imagination is the only limitation when it comes to creating files for output as signage.

Larger signs

If you need a sign that is larger than 8 ¹/₂" x 11", and more finished looking than a laser print, consider Linotronic output— also mounted to foamcore. This creates a sign with a dense black and you can add shades of gray as well. The only drawback is that over time Linotronic output yellows, especially in the sun; but, it should be serviceable for at least a year or two.

1. Check with your service bureau to see how large they can produce Linotronic output. You can create a QuarkXPress publication as large as 48" x 48" (if you do not use double-sided, facing pages) but its height or width should not exceed the dimensions your service bureau can output. You will be limited to a point size no larger than 720 points—which should be enough for most signage.

2. After you create your publication, send it for imagesetting, specifying that crop marks should print, and then follow the procedures outlined in the above section for mounting and trimming. You may wish to use thicker foam-core, ¹/₄", ³/₈" or ¹/₂".

Creating sign templates

If you wish to create a template for painting a window sign, for example, you can create your sign in QuarkXPress, and print it at the percentage size (up to 400% in 1% increments) that will produce the size sign you want. Use the automatic tiling feature and tape the pages together. Tape this tiled sign to the window, and trace over it on the glass. This method is also ideal for signs on cloth or other materials.

Laser printed signs

How often do you see a dog-eared 8 ¹/₂" x 11" laser print—meant to be an attractive and permanent sign—taped on the wall of a waiting area, office, or other public place. With QuarkXPress and a laser printer, you can make handsome, durable signs. Here is how to make signs:

1. Whether you are making just one, or a series of signs, determine a size smaller than 8 ¹/₂" x 11" so that you can print crop marks and trim the page later. This is important.

2. Set page specifications to your desired size— also select a tall or wide page orientation. Usually, wide is a better choice for signs. Choose margins which are equal on the top and sides, with a slightly larger bottom margin.

3. Type your information. Large, bold sans serif fonts make the best signs because they can be read from farther away.

4. Print your sign(s), specifying crop marks on a high-quality laser paper. They can be black on white, black on a colored paper, or printed solid black with reverse type.

5. Using a spray fixative, mount the sign(s) to a piece of ¹/₈" foamcore.

6. Using a sharp blade and a straight edge, trim the sign at the crop marks.

7. Spray the sign with artist's fixative—which will protect it—darken the black and make it slightly shiny.

8. Mount the sign with double-sided tape.

The advent of personal computers and the introduction of programs like QuarkXPress greatly impacted the centuries-old art of typography. Quality type does not just happen. To become a QuarkXPress expert, you must develop a basic understanding of typography, which you can gain from careful study and observation of the typographic world around us.

Fonts are the basis of any QuarkXPress design. Choosing the best typefaces for the job is the beginning. Making them work best is an art.

serif   *sans serif*

This annual report design succeeds in part because of its typographical sophistication. Balance, color, variety, and white space work together to create impact.
Designer: Dorothy A. Cross,
Leimer Cross Design, Seattle
Client: Nintendo Co., Ltd.

Choosing serif or sans serif

Conventional wisdom holds that you read serif typefaces (such as Times Roman, Bodoni, or Palatino) easier than sans serif faces (Helvetica, Futura, Franklin Gothic). When readability is important, use serif faces for body copy. This is because you read text from left to right. The eye scans a group of words, pauses, and then moves on to the next group. The horizontal serifs on the mostly vertical letterforms direct the eye along the horizontal axis.

Sans serif typefaces convey an air of directness with their uncluttered, simple forms. For this reason, they are a good choice for headlines or display text; they impart an immediacy to any message. Because some sans serif faces are very heavy, they read well from a great distance. They also work well when printed in color.

Although the rules for using serif and sans serif faces for body copy and headlines are not steadfast, if you want to break a rule, it's probably better to set headlines in a serif font than to set body text in a sans serif font.

It is seldom advisable to combine two serif or two sans serif fonts in the same document, unless they have markedly different characteristics such as weight, width, or size.

Assessing your fonts

Before you begin your design, determine what fonts you have available and how you can work with them most effectively. Most PostScript laser printers come with a set of basic fonts—usually Avant Garde, Bookman, Courier, Helvetica, Helvetica Narrow, New Century, Palatino, Symbol, Times, Zapf Chancery, and Zapf Dingbats.

If you are limited to a laser printer's basic fonts, you still can create beautiful documents by paying attention to good typography. The list below suggests uses for the basic fonts.

■ Avant Garde

This font can be quite decorative for signage and headlines, but may be a poor choice for body text. Based on the circle, its letterforms have an open, airy feeling. Avant Garde is a good font to condense or extend.

AVANT GARDE:
Cool and aloof.

■ Bookman

Bookman bold is ideal for headlines and can be used for body text in its lighter version. It has a friendly, informal feeling. Because of its wide characters, it is not very economical for getting a lot of copy into a small space.

Bookman is warm
and friendly.

■ Courier

Use Courier when you want your publication to look like it was created on a typewriter. Because Courier does not have proportional spacing, each character takes up the same amount of space—whether it is a W or an I.

```
If you want your
publication to look
like it was typewritten,
Courier is the right
choice.
```

■ Helvetica

Based on a design originally created for London Underground signage in the 1800s, Helvetica gained popularity in the 1950s for its balance and purity of form. After its introduction, it became very popular—almost too much so. It is sometimes used without much thought simply because it is considered a safe choice.

Helvetica makes good signage and headlines—especially its bold version. Generally, it is not a good choice for body text.

HELVETICA:
Classic form.

■ Helvetica Narrow

Many laser printers come with the Helvetica Narrow font. It is not recommended for body text because it is difficult to read, but it makes great headlines when it is set in a large point size.

Originally, Helvetica Narrow had no high-resolution equivalent for Linotronic output. This caused great confusion when it was used in place of Condensed Helvetica. When files were sent for imagesetting, the font could not be printed because it is not possible to convert Narrow Helvetica to Helvetica Condensed.

■ New Century

An overlooked gem, New Century, is a face with beautiful impact when used as display type. At the same time, it can be very effective as body text. Its school book origin makes the reader feel comfortable instantly and its straightforward simplicity makes it ideal for books and manuals.

Look Sally! See Spot.
New Century makes it
easy to read.

Watch the beautiful Palatino Italic "dance" across a page.

■ **Palatino**

Palatino was modeled from type found carved in stone in Roman ruins. Its classical elegance conveys an air of conservatism, solidity, and grace. (Think of publications for banks, churches, or foundations.)

Palatino has a beautiful italic face—one that dances across a page. This italic is an appropriate choice for lead-ins, pull quotes, or captions.

■ **Symbol**

Use Symbol for mathematical equations and technical documents.

$$\alpha\beta\chi\delta\epsilon\phi\gamma\eta\iota\phi\kappa\lambda$$
$$\mu\nu o\pi\theta\rho\sigma\tau\upsilon\varpi\omega\xi\psi\zeta$$

■ **Times**

Derived from a design originated by *The London Times* (circa 1850), to get the most legible text into the smallest amount of space, Times succeeds today as a versatile face. It combines formal elegance with business-like conviction. Times is an excellent choice for body text because of its economy. It also makes a particularly beautiful display face—conveying an image of strength, order, and clarity.

■ **Zapf Chancery**

Script fonts have a calligraphic or hand-written feeling. They give a feeling of elegance and ease. Zapf Chancery, the only script font in the basic laser printer group, is good for invitations and other informal uses. In a large point size, it makes interesting initial caps. When skewed or stretched, its calligraphic forms are emphasized. This font is extremely hard to read in all caps.

See how dramatic Zapf Chancery can be when it's skewed and rotated?

■ **Zapf Dingbats**

This effective type provides emphasis to a statement or a decorative treatment. However, dingbats must be used with care: too many on a page create a cluttered look.

If you're uncertain where to find a particular Zapf Dingbat, select Key Caps under the Apple menu. It works like this:

1. Under the Apple menu, pull down and release on Key Caps. Key Caps then appears as a choice on the menu bar

2. Pull down Key Caps from the menu bar, and choose Zapf Dingbats from the pull-down menu.

3. The keyboard onscreen shows the Zapf Dingbat characters. Pressing the Shift key, the Option key, or the Shift and Option keys together will display the Zapf Dingbats available through those combinations.

4. Clicking on the screen keyboard characters places the Zapf Dingbat character(s) in the window above the keyboard. Select the character(s); perform the copy and paste functions. When you return to QuarkXPress paste your copied character(s) into your document. (You then must select your pasted character(s) and change the font to Zapf Dingbats when you are in the QuarkXPress document.)

5. You also can type in a character in Layout, select it and change its font to Zapf Dingbat.

Times isn't often considered for headlines, but it makes good ones.

Avoid fonts with a city name

Unless you want to deliberately create stair-stepped bitmap images for a modern, computerized look, avoid the city-name fonts: New York, Chicago, Monaco, etc. These are Macintosh computer fonts originally designed only for screen display and ImageWriter printers. When you print these fonts you will get stair-stepped bitmap images. Smooth versions of these fonts usually cannot be printed through high-resolution imagesetting.

Adding fonts

Most professional designers buy additional fonts—and there are numerous ones from which to choose. Your personal preferences will determine what you buy. Font packages range in price from a few dollars to two or three hundred dollars each. Before you purchase a font, make sure that your service bureau can output that font.

Downloaded fonts

Fonts that you purchase and add to your system must be downloaded to your printer—hence the name. This is not a difficult technical maneuver (refer to your documentation). What is more difficult is choosing from the thousands of fonts available.

Here are some personal favorites you may consider when building a foundation for your font library:

■ **Serif**

Bodoni, Cheltenham, Garamond, Garamond Condensed, Goudy, New Baskerville

■ **Sans Serif**

Futura, Futura Condensed, Helvetica Black, Helvetica Compressed, Helvetica Condensed, Univers, Franklin Gothic

■ **Script**

Shelley, Brush Script, Park Avenue

■ **Other**

Sumner Stone's Adobe font, Stone provides serif, sans serif, and informal faces—all of which you can use together effectively. (This book is set in Stone.)

Some sources for fonts

Adobe Systems
(800) 83-FONTS

Agfa
(800) 424-8973

Autologic
(800) 457-8973

Bitstream
(800) 237-3553

Casady & Greene
(408) 484-9228

Digital Typeface Corporation
(612) 944-9264

Emigre
(800) 944-9021

The Font Company
(602) 998-9711

FontHaus, Inc.
(800) 942-9110

Fonts West
(415) 777-3011

ImageClub Graphics
(403) 262-8008

International Typeface Corp. (ITC)
(212) 371-0699

Letraset
(800) 343-TYPE

Linotype
(800) 633-1900

Monotype
(800) MONOTYPE

NEC Technologies
(800) 826-2255

Choosing the right typeface and its speci-fications are critical design decisions. Remember that readability comes first. Choose point sizes, weight, leading, line length, alignment, colors, and other attributes with care.

Text alignment

QuarkXPress's text handling capabilities allow for left aligned, centered, right aligned, justified, and force justified text. There are rules for choosing these options, too.

■ Left aligned

The most readable choice for body text is left aligned. Its consistent word spac-ing and varying rag along the right-hand side make it easier for the eye to track from the end of one line to the beginning of the next. Left-aligned text combines a no-nonsense look with modern informality, yielding a sensible, straightforward feeling.

Centered text can be more effective when it's emphasized, given lots of attention, and space.

■ Centered

Centered text is more formal. Use it for headlines, pull-quotes, and other display situations. In QuarkXPress, be careful where you locate the text block han-dles—or the text may be centered with-in its block, not the column or the page. Also, avoid using indents and tabs when centering text; they may throw off lines in relation to one another.

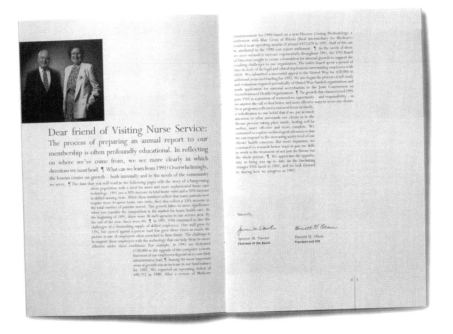

Dear friend of Visiting Nurse Service:

The brochure at the left illustrates deliberate and effective use of type alignment. The arrangement follows a subtle step theme used throughout the publication.
Designers: Laura Lacy-Sholly & James Sholly
Antenna, Indianapolis
Client: The Visiting Nurse Association

■ Right aligned

Because right-aligned text is contrary to how we read, use it very sparingly. It works in special applications such as captions on the left of a photo or illustration, or as a large-size introductory phrase or paragraph at the beginning of an article.

Lorem ipsum dolor sit amet, consecteteur adipiscing elit, sed diam nonummy nibh euismod tincidunt ut laoreet dolore magna aliquam erat volutpat. Ut wisi enim as minim veniam, quis nostrud exerci tation ullamcorper suscipit lobortis nisl ut aliquip ex ae commodo consequat. Duis autem vel eum iriure dolor in hendrer.

Right aligned text makes an interesting lead-in to a paragraph of body text if it's treated like this.

■ Justified

This text treatment is formal, yet commonplace in magazines and newspapers. It brings strict order to a page. If you choose it for body copy, handle it carefully. Justifying text is more tricky than most people realize. Unless you achieve the right balance between point size and column width, you may end up with too few words on a line, creating exaggerated spaces between words. Justified text also requires that you pay close attention to hyphenation. Too many lines ending with hyphens is tiresome and jarring: too few hyphenated words will create uneven word spacing.

This column is too narrow for justified type this size; as a result, it looks awkward and unbalanced.

■ Force justified

Force justified text is like justified, except that the last line of a paragraph is justified—even if it contains only a few characters. When used with words of similar length, it can give a stylish appearance. Often, it can create a hard to read, self-conscious design. Use sparingly.

FORCE JUSTIFIED TEXT
CAN BE VERY STYLISH

Point sizes and column widths

Point size should relate to column width. If point size is too large, words cannot form enough groups on a short line that the eye needs for efficient reading. If line lengths are too long and filled with small type, the eye can lose its place reading from the end of one line to the beginning of the next. Generally, your column is too narrow if it contains fewer than 8 words; more than 20 words may result in a column that it is too wide. Once again, this isn't a steadfast rule, rather a rule of thumb made to be broken if the situation warrants.

This column is too wide for type this small, unless it's for some kind of contract where you want to make the fine print hard to read. If there are many justified lines of this length, it is easy for the reader to get lost when scanning from the end of one line to the beginning of the next.

Font styles

Most fonts contain a bold, italic, and bold italic version. Some, such as Avant Garde shown on the right, have even more weights. Together these versions make up a font family. The font designer created each version with its own defining characteristics. When using QuarkXPress, if your bold or italic printer fonts are not found, you can choose a bold or italic style for text that will yield a system generated bold or italic. These fattened or obliqued versions of the original face are not the true bold or italic. As clumsy as it may seem, you should select the proper font, (e.g., B Garamond Bold), rather than simply checking Bold in a dialog box.

You can alleviate this situation, however, by installing a utility that combines your font families—such as Adobe Type Reunion. Once you organize the fonts as a family, you can select the proper bold face with Command-B, and italic with Command-I. Until you install this utility, continue to do the typographically correct thing and select the true face each time you use it.

Avant Garde Extra Light

Extra Light Oblique

Avant Garde Book

Book Oblique

Avant Garde Medium

Medium Oblique

Avant Garde Demi

Demi Oblique

Avant Garde Bold

Bold Oblique

Bodoni Regular

Bodoni Italic

Bodoni Bold

Bodoni Bold Italic

Transforming Type

One of the most exciting features QuarkXPress offers the designer is the power to transform type. It is simple to expand or compress type, providing opportunities for abstraction and looking at the conventional in fresh ways. This power also carries the potential to create distortions of carefully configured letterforms, and many design and typography purists object to it. In spite of that, transformed type has become a hallmark of electronic publishing design.

You can transform type by going into the Character specs menu and altering Horizontal width to a different percentage size. (The default is 100%.) The F in the figure above has been compressed to 25 percent of its normal width.

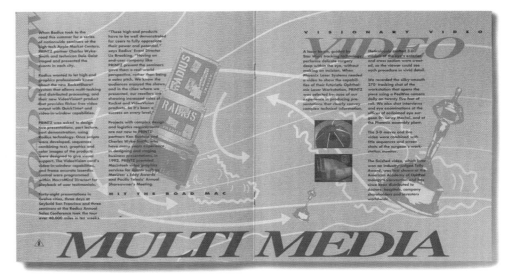

This brochure's type was expanded to 120% to emphasize the electronic production capabilities of the company.
Designer: Mike Bertoni
Cleint: PRINTZ Electronic Design

Reverses

Sometimes the eye seeks something different. The term "reverse" denotes a total opposite in terms of color—from positive to negative. Like anything else, reversed type can be very effective if it is done well. Here are some guidelines to follow:

■ Be careful not to use a typeface with thin letter strokes. These can fill in when printed because of dot gain or other ink coverage problems.

■ Avoid using small point sizes unless the typeface is really bold.

■ You can use reversed type as visual dividers to indicate a section or subsection of a publication.

■ Carefully consider the framing for your reversed type. Keep an adequate border of solid color around the type. Also note how the solid background works in the context of the entire page. Is it more dominant than the type inside it? Should it be?

■ In books (such as this one) reverses can double as thumb tabs when they bleed off the edge of the page.

Creating reverses as a style

If your publication has many instances that call for the same treatment of information in a reverse bar, define a Style by following the steps below. You will save time and achieve perfect measurement where you apply the style.

1. Type a word or phrase. Make certain its type specifications are correct. Change the type color to white.

2. Use the Text tool to select the text; choose Rules from the Style menu.

3. Select Top rule. Define the thickness, making it a least as thick as the point size of the type. Decide if you want the rules to be the width of the text or the width of the indents. (Width of indents is better because it provides consistency in repetitive visual elements on the page.) Choose a color for the rule and define its offset.

4. Select bottom rule and repeat the steps as outlined in number three.

5. Click apply to check the offset of the rules. Modify as necessary then click on the OK button.

All caps and small caps

Setting type in all caps can create emphasis. However, if you use all caps (even for a headline) you can make it harder to read your message—not easier. This is because the variation found in upper and lower case letters helps the eye track across the text. In most instances, using all caps for body text is inappropriate.

Small caps will substitute upper case letters for those that normally would be lower case, (in a smaller point size than the letters would be if they were capitalized). When used for small amounts of text, such as headlines or pull quotes, small caps can add a refined look to a publication. If used as body text, small caps look contrived and are hard to read.

Applying colors to type

You can print type in spot color or in process colors. If you wish to assign a color to letters or words, simply use the Text tool from the Toolbox, select the desired text, and choose the color from the color palette. (See page 34 for a discussion of spot vs. process color.)

Use color type carefully. Headlines in a second color usually carry less emphasis than they do in full black. Body text becomes more difficult to read. Pull quotes, drop caps, and similar lead-ins are appropriate candidates for colorizing.

LOREM IPSUM DOLOR SIT AMET, CONSECTETUER ADIPISCING ELIT, SED DIAM NONUMMY NIBH EUISMOD TINCIDUNT UT LAOREET DOLORE MAGNA ALIQUAM ERAT VOLUTPAT. UT WISI ENIM AD MINIM VENIAM, QUIS NOSTRUD EXEERCI TATION ULLAMCORPER SUSCIPIT

LOREM IPSUM DOLOR SIT AMET, CONSECTETUER ADIPISCING ELIT, SED DIAM NONUMMY NIBH EUISMOD TINCIDUNT UT LAOREET DOLORE MAGNA ALIQUAM ERAT VOLUTPAT. UT WISI ENIM AD MINIM VENIAM, QUIS NOSTRUD EXERCI TATION ULLAMCORPER SUSCIPIT

Notice the difference between type set in all caps on the left, and small caps on the right. Both text blocks contain the same words, set in the same point size.

The Character... menu

When I first saw this menu in QuarkXPress, I fell in love then and there with the program. Realizing the potential to easily change the characteristics of all the text in a document, I learned quickly that Command+Shift+D can bring nearly instant gratification.

The Characteristic menu offers a pull-down shortcut when you want to change a single characteristic of type, such as its font, size, etc.

Character Attributes

Font: ▶ 1Stone Serif

Size: ▶ 18 pt

Color: White

Shade: ▶ 100%

Style
- ☒ Plain
- ☐ Bold
- ☐ Italic
- ☐ Outline
- ☐ Shadow
- ☐ Strike Thru
- ☐ Underline
- ☐ Word u.l.
- ☐ Small Caps
- ☐ All Caps
- ☐ Superscript
- ☐ Subscript

Horizontal Scale: 100%

Kern Amount: 0

Baseline Shift: 0 pt

[OK]   [Cancel]

The Character...attributes dialog box.

Style
- Font ▶
- Size ▶
- Type Style ▶
- Color ▶
- Shade ▶
- Horizontal Scale...
- Kern...
- Baseline Shift...
- Character... ⌘⇧D
- Alignment ▶
- Leading... ⌘⇧E
- Formats... ⌘⇧F
- Rules... ⌘⇧N
- Tabs... ⌘⇧T
- Style Sheets ▶

The Style pull-down menu is where you access Character specifications. Character...contains a combined list of all the options that you can apply to text.

The full Style menu is much more than just a place to change a font or point size. Let's look at some of its features:

■ Font

This is where you select the proper font for your text. Using the Text tool, you must select your text first to change the currently selected font.

■ Size

In QuarkXPress, you can specify type sizes from 4 to 720 points. Clicking on the arrow to the right of the Size box, you can quickly choose preset sizes for selected text. However, if you wish to assign a size not on the list, (such as 33 point), or sizes in $1/10$ point increments, you will need to enter a specific number in the dialog box. You do this by choosing Other and then typing in your new size.

■ Type style

Click Italic, Bold, Underline, etc. to change type style. If you select a bold font, such as B Garamond Bold, do not assign the bold attribute to it in the Character attributes box. Likewise, do not choose italic this way for a font such as Goudy italic.

■ Color

This little menu serves the same function as the Color palette. Determining your types color while choosing other type specifications is very convenient. Clicking on the Color box and dragging down reveals your choices.

■ Horizontal Scale

This is one way to expand or compress type. You can make type as wide as 400% of the normal value, or as narrow as 25%. Remember, changing the width affects the type's readability and purity of form, and if done on large amounts of type will significantly slow down screen refreshes of that text.

Kern Amount

Kerning controls how loose or tight individual letters are in relation to one another. Under Kern you can set the amount anywhere from -500 to +500. Kerning affects larger point sizes more than it does smaller ones. When you apply kerning to type, you should run laser proofs until you are happy with how the type looks. Kerning can have a very dramatic impact.

Baseline Shift

Baseline shift can be a very functional tool. It offers you the flexibility to shift type either above or below other characters with the same line of text. The amount of shift can range from -54 to +54 points.

Formats

The Formats menu, found in the Style pull-down menu, can set indents and alignment. I find its greatest use is in creating extra space between paragraphs. Using global functions such as format styles in conjunction with features like extra paragraph spacing give documents the consistency that marks professional work.

Adding space between paragraphs

Using this option, you do not need to insert extra carriage returns between paragraphs. You also can ensure that headlines or subheads are always followed by the correct amount of spacing before body text begins. To add extra space before or after a paragraph, follow these steps:

1. Place your cursor in a paragraph and access the Paragraph Formats submenu from the Style menu, or type Command+Shift+F.

2. It's most useful to use points and picas for measurement. In the dialog box under Space after, type the desired amount of space in picas. You can use points too. (Remember, 6 picas equals one inch; there are twelve points to a pica. Therefore, 1p6 would mean 1 pica and 6 points, or 1 $\frac{1}{2}$ picas. These points are the same points used to measure type, so if you are using 10 point type on 12 point leading, one pica (12 points) between paragraphs would be the same space as one carriage return.)

3. Click on the OK button. Now, each time you type a return to end one paragraph and begin a new one, the new one will begin the correct distance away from the preceding paragraph.

Breaking paragraphs

Another useful function of the Paragraph Formats submenu is its capability to control where paragraphs break. You can specify that lines stay together, begin a column, or begin a new page.

Paragraph Rules

You also can create paragraph styles that have rules above and below text; and, rules that have specific weights, colors, and vertical distances away from text blocks.

Paragraph Formats	
Left Indent: 0"	Leading: auto
First Line: 0"	Space Before: 0"
Right Indent: 0"	Space After: 1p6
☐ Lock to Baseline Grid	☐ Keep with Next ¶
☐ Drop Caps	☐ Keep Lines Together
Alignment: Left	Apply
H&J: Standard	OK Cancel

Letter, word, line, and paragraph spacing are all very important design considerations. An understanding of how spacing works will help you achieve greater control working with type.

Letter spacing by kerning

In QuarkXPress you can adjust the space between letters. Letter spacing, or kerning, can be set manually or automatically under the Tracking attributes menu. Kerning type means increasing or decreasing the space between characters to achieve a more even fit between pairs of letters. To kern, QuarkXPress measures each letter's distance from the letter preceding it as a percentage of the word space (the distance entered when you press the space bar, known as an em space).

You can apply Automatic pair kerning on the Formats style palette. This will change every kern pair in an entire paragraph. With a paragraph selected, or as you define a style, select kern amount in the Character Attributes dialog box under the Style menu.

Sometimes it is desirable to use Quark's default kerning, particularly if you cannot remember what manual kerning you have applied to a word, or group of words. You can do this by selecting a range of text and entering 0 for the tracking percentage on the Measurements palette.

Typographic Preferences for Bleeds

Superscript
Offset: 33%
VScale: 100%
HScale: 100%

Subscript
Offset: 33%
VScale: 100%
HScale: 100%

Baseline Grid
Start: 0.5"
Increment: 12 pt

Auto Leading: 20%
Flex Space Width: 50%
☒ Auto Kern Above: 10 pt
☒ Maintain Leading

Small Caps
VScale: 75%
HScale: 75%

Superior
VScale: 50%
HScale: 50%

Ligatures: Off   1
Hyphenation Method: Enhanced
Character Widths: Fractional
Leading Mode: Typesetting

OK   Cancel

WAVE
7.
1994

WAVE
7.
1994

In the examples above, the red type illustrates typical kerning problems. The blue type shows improved kerning by tightening the spaces between certain characters.

■ Word Spacing

While it is possible to change word spacing, doing so deviates from the font designer's ideal spacing. There is little reason for changing word spacing unless you are trying to clean up a text block by bringing up a single word from another line, or you want to reduce hyphenation in justified text.

■ Line spacing

Line spacing can be a very effective design tool. It imparts a rhythm to a page. You can control Line spacing through the Leading feature in the Style menu.

■ Leading

Leading is the technical term for line spacing. Increased leading creates more space between lines; decreased leading creates less space between lines. In QuarkXPress there are four settings for positioning text within its leading (see illustration below). You can find them by choosing Modify under the Item menu and selecting your option from the Vertical Alignment palette.

Duis autem vel eum iriure dolor in hendrerit in vulputate.

Vertical Alignment set to top.

Duis autem vel eum iriure dolor in hendrerit in vulputate.

Vertical Alignment set to centered.

Duis autem vel eum iriure dolor in hendrerit in vulputate.

Vertical Alignment set to bottom.

Duis autem vel eum iriure dolor in hendrerit in vulputate.

Vertical Alignment set to justified.

■ Spacing between sentences

Many typists and word processors instinctively place two spaces between sentences. This is contrary to typesetting conventions that call for only one space. (Otherwise, you invite "rivers" of white space flowing down your columns.) You can use the Find/Change command under the Edit menu, to search and replace double spaces with single spaces. Even if you input the text yourself, it is always possible that you may have entered two spaces here or there. You'll be happier finding them before you output your files than after your document is printed.

Importing

QuarkXPress can place text in your document from many different sources: typewritten pages, Macintosh word-processing files, and text files from DOS and Windows platforms. Correctly importing text is very important in the production process.

Typewritten or printed text

If the copy for your design comes from typewritten or printed pages, instead of an electronic file—you can have the pages scanned using an Optical Character Recognition (OCR) software program and a scanner to save time. Once scanned, the text can be saved in a common word-processing format and then edited in QuarkXPress. Although these programs can be difficult to use, many service bureaus can do the scanning for you. This is a good solution if there is a large amount of text to enter.

Text from word processing programs

QuarkXPress can import text from numerous word processing programs—including Microsoft Word, Microsoft Works, WordPerfect, and others, from both Macintosh and PC platforms if you have an active filter for your particular word processing program.

There are many ways to get text from a PC into QuarkXPress on your Macintosh. All recent Macintosh models since the release of the SE-30 model, include a disk drive that reads PC disks using Apple File Exchange. There is also conversion hardware (such as disk drives from Dayna) and software (such as MacLink). You also can send text files over a modem from a PC to a Macintosh, in which case you will need to use ASCII, or the text only format. Transferring files using the ASCII format results in losing the majority of the file's formatting.

Style sheet characteristics

If you can retain the file's formatting when converting a PC word processing file or importing a Macintosh file, styling characteristics such as character (bold, italic), paragraph (spacing, indents), and style attributes (font, point size, leading) will be imported into the QuarkXPress document and will not need to be reapplied.

Style-name tags

When preparing text in a text only, or ASCII word-processing program, you can add style-name tags at the beginning of each paragraph that you import into QuarkXPress and want interpreted as a style. This means that text created with a word processing program can be assigned styles, even if the program does not support paragraph style definitions. The designations look like this: <headline>, <body text>, etcetera. Place the tags at the beginning of each paragraph that requires a change in style. There can be no characters or spaces preceding them. A tag that contains no name (< >) will be treated as if it has no assigned style.

QuarkXPress will apply the style to the paragraph that follows the tag and to all subsequent paragraphs, until it finds a different style-name tag.

When importing documents with style-name tags, use Get Text under the File menu, and check the Include Style Sheets option. The style-name tag must match a style already defined in the QuarkXPress file before importing the text.

From database/spreadsheet programs

Spreadsheet files created in Excel and Lotus 1-2-3 formats can be imported as text into QuarkXPress. When you import text from a database or spreadsheet program, it may require extensive formatting in QuarkXPress because style attributes from the original program are sometimes lost.

You generally will want to export spreadsheets as tab delimited text, (which means that a tab will be inserted between the data in each cell). This makes formatting the data using the Indents/tabs feature in QuarkXPress easier.

For specific information about how to export spreadsheet and database files as text, refer to the manuals for those programs.

From other QuarkXPress publications

When importing text from one QuarkXPress file into another, open both files, click on the text block you want to copy with the Pointer tool, and drag it to the new file. This will copy the text displayed in the first file into the new one.

Other times, you can open one QuarkXPress file, select all the text in one story by placing the Text tool cursor in the text block, select all (Command-A) and copy (Command-C). When you open the new file, select the Text tool, click the cursor on the page and paste (Command-V). The text retains its specifications.

Headlines are important in the design of any publication. Although headlines may vary from article to article, they provide an underlying consistency in your design. Usually, headlines contrast with body text in size, color, weight, font choice, or placement.

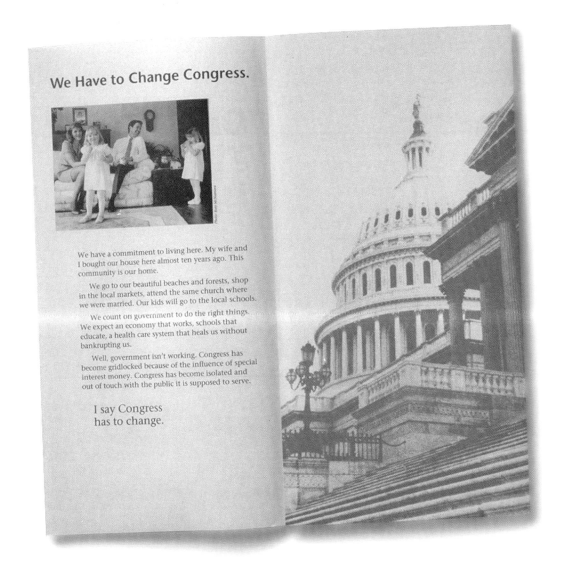

The headline, "We Have to Change Congress," is the focal point of this campaign brochure. Designer: Michael J. Nolan Client: Joe Nation for Congress Committee

Headline uses

Headlines grab attention. They must be well-written, succinct, and easy to read. The amount of contrast between the headline and the body text is an important design decision.

You can achieve contrast using different techniques: color, font selection, point size, weight, or placement. Choose one or two techniques and apply them consistently throughout your publication.

- Use a color headline above black body text.

- Use a different, much bolder font in the same or even smaller point size.

- Use a different point size featuring a larger, but lighter face for the headline.

- Span all the columns of an article with its headline.

- Indent or outdent the headline.

- Rotate the headline, or insert it into the body text.

- Use stepping down type—a very old technique—that can lead from headline to body text.

Bolder, 1 point smaller & different font

Lorem ipsum dolor sit amet, consectetuer adipiscing elit, sed diam non ummy nibh euismod tincidunt. Ut laoreet dolore magna aliquam erat volutpat.

Lighter font larger point size, another color.

Ut wisi enim as minim veniam, quis nostrud exerci. Tation ullamcorper suscipit lobortis nisl ut aliquip ex ea commodo consequat. Hendrerit in vulputate velit esse molestie consequat, vel illum dolore eu feugiat nulla facilisis at cero eros et accumsan et iusto odio dignissim qui blandit praesent luptatum zzril delenit augue duis dolore te feu gait nulla facilisi.

This is an example of the very old, but very useful stepping down type technique.

Lorem ipsum dolor sit amet, consectetuer adipiscing elit, sed diam non ummy nibh euismod tincidunt. Ut laoreet dolore magna aliquam erat volutpat. Ut wisi enim as minim veniam, quis nostrud exerci. Tation ullamcorper suscipit lobortis nisl ut aliquip ex ea commodo consequat. Hendrerit in vulputate velit esse molestie consequat.

An Outdented Headline Works Well

Ut wisi enim as minim veniam, quis nostrud exerci. Tation ullamcorper suscipit lobortis nisl ut aliquip ex ea commodo consequat. Hendrerit in vulputate velit esse molestie consequat, vel illum dolore eu feugiat nulla facilisis at cero eros et accumsan et iusto odio dignissim.

Headline guidelines

There are many ways to ensure the best use of headlines:

- Limit the number of headline treatments and ensure that you apply the treatments consistently by using style definitions.

- Coordinate headlines with subheads by deriving subheads from either headline or body text fonts.

- Avoid all caps in headlines; they can be hard to read. Writers often use all caps for headlines as they type. You may need to rekey headline text if heads are in all caps.

- Avoid the underline type style. If you set underlined words in headlines, they look clunky and are hard to read, thereby giving the headline less emphasis. If you must underline, use paragraph rules or the Line tool in QuarkXPress and control the weight, color, and placement of the underscoring.

- Don't use too many fonts, sizes, or colors. If you treat every headline differently, the reader cannot establish a visual hierarchy to determine the most important articles. The publication takes on a messy, jumbled appearance.

- Be careful how you handle rules and other column conventions. If a headline spans three columns and there is a rule between each column of text, the inside rules must stop at the same level.

- Subheads break up text into subsections, and carry almost as much impact as headlines. Be sure that the subheads are compatible with body text and headlines.

- Ensure every headline is set the same distance from the top of its column, and that the measurement of all body text from its headline is the same. Pay attention to whether the measurement from headline to first paragraph is the same, more, or less than that between paragraphs. Keep the application of styles consistent. This is where Quark's Paragraph Formats specifications menu in conjunction with style definitions really helps.

1. With a headline selected, choose Formats from the Style menu.

2. Choose the amount of space below the headline by entering a value in the After box. (If your measurement preferences are different than the measurement system you want to use, type your measurement as .5 for $\frac{1}{2}$ inch, or 0p4 for 4 points.)

3. With the text selected, choose Style Sheets from the Edit menu. It should have Normal highlighted, now click on New. This will give you an opportunity to name the selected style. You can type in Headline and replace the existing headline style.

4. Each time you select a line of text and style it as headline, the body text begins the correct distance below.

Avoid the Underline Type Style

Instead, Draw Your Own Line

HEADLINES IN ALL CAPS CAN BE HARD TO READ

Headlines Not in All Caps Can Be Easier to Read

Measure All Rules Between Columns When a Headline Spans Several

Ut wisi enim as minim veniam, quis nostrud exerci. Tation ullamcorper suscipit lobortis nisl ut aliquip ex ea commodo consequat. Hendrerit in vulputate velit esse molestie consequat, vel illum dolore eu feugiat nulla facilisis at cero eros et accum-

san et iusto odio dignissim qui blandit praesent luptatum zzril delenit augue duis dolore te feu gait nulla facilisi.Ut wisi enim as minim veniam, quis nostrud exerci. Tation ullamcorper suscipit lobortis nisl ut aliquip ex ea commodo consequat.

Hendrerit in vulputate velit esse molestie consequat, vel illum dolore eu feugiat nulla facilisis at cero eros et accumsan et iusto odio dignissim qui blandit praesent luptatum zzril delenit augue duis dolore te feu gait nulla facilisi.

The use of initial caps dates back hundreds of years to when monks created illuminated manuscripts. More than simply beautiful, they help organize information and provide an additional point of entry that leads the reader into the text.

Katie is tall, slender, aristocratic looking, though she is wholly without pomp and affectation. From a photograph one might guess her to be upper-tier European royalty, but only if she isn't smiling. A laugh will shatter the illusion quickly. A true royal never would open up the way Katie does with a laugh. She is, she says, "Just a stubborn Austrian." The blood is red, not blue. And Katie is in love. Stubborn Austrian love.

Bernie is all scrubbed, bright-eyed, ruddy-faced Irish. From a photo, smiling or not, one would always guess him to be Irish. No chance for royalty here, though somehow it's easy to imagine a leprechaun perched on a branch of the family tree. He speaks in short bursts, Irish laconic it is called, usually in sentences no longer than the snap count for the Notre Dame quarterback. He rarely seems unhappy, save for golf games lost at the 18th hole, and the central reason is the tall, smiling Austrian he married 50 years ago. 🌹

Katie's Prayer

Upon the occasion of their Golden Wedding Anniversary, Katie wrote this:

When I was about 20 years old I started praying to Saint Anthony to find me a good husband. As it happened, he chose Bun Doyle. That was his nickname at the time. They couldn't have found a better husband than Bernie. He was everything one could ask for and then more. Seeing and meeting Bernie for the first time was at a Catholic Youth Young Adults houseparty. I couldn't take my eyes off him that night and haven't since.

We became engaged at Christmas of 1940 and were married April 19, 1941, at the St. Joe Farm Parish by Father Murray.

He had just been ordained a few years before that.

I said, "Dear Lord, bless us with a beautiful daughter," which we are thankful for.

We have truly enjoyed our first 50 years together and have many, many, many lovely memories of them. The hard work, the good times, the nice travel, the vacations, the years of playing golf. May this be the year Bernie can score his age in golf and not let opponents run in long putts on number 18 to win the tournament of the day.

Besides loving God, I wonder if golf is his first or second love.

We are very proud of our lovely family, relatives, and friends. Also the wonderful clergy we have been associated with over the years. May the dear Lord bless us with continued health and happiness. We have so much to be thankful for.

Amen

The Meeting

There is no question who the romantic is in the family. About the day he met Katie, Bernie remembers, "We met at a party. We were on and off for awhile." And was he, as one might suppose he would be upon seeing the person who would be his partner for half a century, immediately struck by the vision of Katie?

"Oh, yeah," chuckles Bernie. "I suppose."

And what were his thoughts that day? "That's a hard question. I don't remember back 50 years like that."

That's okay. Katie does. The year was 1939. The year of Rhett and Scarlett. And Katie and Bernie.

"We used to have what you'd call the CYO. Everyone would meet at someone else's home. We were at this big houseparty. Everyone played cards at a certain table. I was sitting in a big dining room. Bernie came in late because he always had to milk cows three times a day in those years.

"When he came in, he just really took my eye, you know. I thought, 'Boy, I wonder who

This brochure, celebrating a couple's 50th wedding anniversary, uses initial caps in the Shelley Allegro font to begin each section of text.
Designer: Michael J. Nolan

There are many ways to design initial caps. Here are some thoughts about creating them:

- Don't be timid when creating initial caps. They are extravagant by nature and should be large enough in relation to the body text to really stand out. An initial cap only two text lines high is usually not effective.

- Give initial caps room to breathe. Don't set them too close to headlines or they will look crowded.

- Measure initial caps carefully. Initial caps touching the letters that follow them, or those too far away, are clumsy and show inattention to detail. The same is true of caps that hover above or below the baseline of the body text. Check your spacing using 200% or 400% magnification. Be prepared to print out several laser proofs until you get it right.

- If you are printing only black, consider using a screen value for the initial cap.

- Combine fonts. Mix serif and sans serif faces. Use scripts and other specialty fonts that would not work for body text or headlines.

- Transform letters by stretching, rotating, or other type manipulations that will draw attention to the initial cap—which is what it's supposed to do.

- Certain rounded letters, such as the S, O or Q should sit slightly below the baseline of the body text because of the illusion created by the curve.

- Try different methods of placement. Some initial caps can stand on the baseline of the first line of text and tower above; others can be embedded or dropped several lines down into the text. They also can be outdented or indented. (Whatever style you choose, however, ensure that you apply that style consistently throughout the publication.)

Exaggerated letters, such as this Univers Extra Black E condensed to 20% of its usual width can provide interesting variations from the ordinary. In addition, this initial cap is colored yellow and set in a purple box, which gives it even more impact, especially when contrasted against the red color of the body text.

This text block illustrates centered type with an initial cap.

Creating initial caps

Using QuarkXPress, you can create initial caps as part of the body text block, or as a separate text block. They can be imported EPS files, TIFF, or PICT scans that you wrap text around, or they can be made using the Drop Caps option under the Paragraph Formats submenu. No particular method is best for all situations. Let's look at some different ways you can create initial caps:

■ Standing caps as part of a text block

When you create initial caps within a text block, the key to success is proper leading. Use the steps below to create standing caps:

1. Make sure you are working in Proportional leading.

2. With the Type tool, select the first character of the first word in the text block, and open Characteristics... (Command+Shift+T). Change the point size to a larger specification. You also can change the font or style, but not the leading.

3. You may have to kern the body text in the first word closer to or farther from the initial cap. Click between the initial cap and the next letter, and either increase or decrease the amount of tracking.

■ Drop caps as a separate text block

Drop caps can be created either through the Drop cap option... or by using two text blocks. The first way is easier; but the second way offers more control. Here's how to make a drop cap three lines deep using two text blocks:

1. Flow the text block into the column, draw down a guideline to line four, close the window until only three lines appear. Use the lower left handle to move the left margin enough to accommodate the drop cap.

2. Create another text block and link the first block to the second. Next position the new text box so that the first line of text aligns with the guide you placed.

3. Cut the first letter from the first word (Command-X). Paste the letter into this new text block (Command-V); select it, and open Type Characteristics... (Command+Shift+D) to change its specifications.

4. Change to 200% view; use the Pointer tool on the left-hand bottom handle of the first three lines of text to adjust it closer to or away from the drop cap.

5. Use the Pointer tool to adjust the guideline to the baseline of the third line of type. Click on the drop cap and adjust it vertically until it shares the same baseline.

◼ Imported letters, scans or drawings

You also can create initial caps in programs such as Aldus FreeHand or Adobe Illustrator, or they can be scanned images saved in TIFF or PICT formats. Use these methods when you want an elaborate, multicolored letter that incorporates graphics. They are also good for creating initial caps that lie underneath the text rather than beside it.

*I*orem ipsum dolor sit amet, consectetuer adipiscing elit, sed diam non ummy nibh euismod tincidunt. Ut laoreet dolore magna aliquam erat volutpat.

The initial cap in this example was created in Aldus Freehand with a 20% fill. Then it was imported into QuarkXPress, and placed behind the text.

1 Duis autem vel eum iriure dolor in hendrerit in vulputate vetit esse molestie consequat, vel illum dolore eu feugiat nulla facilisis at vero eros et accumsan et iusto odio dignissim qui blandit

2 Paragraph Formats

Left Indent: 0
First Line: 0"
Right Indent: 0"
☐ Lock to Baseline Grid
☒ Drop Caps
3 Character Count: 1
Line Count: 3

Leading: auto
Space Before: 0"
Space After: 0"
☐ Keep with Next ¶
☐ Keep Lines Together
○ All Lines in ¶
○ Start: 2 End: 2

Alignment: Left
H&J: Standard

Apply
OK   Cancel

◼ Automated drop caps

The Drop caps option under the Paragraph Formats menu provides a simple solution if you are using drop caps repeatedly throughout a publication. It is routine and does not involve as much careful measurement as other methods. Here's how it works:

1. Using the Text tool, select the letter for the drop cap.

2. Go to the Paragraph Formats submenu under the Style menu and select Drop Caps.

3. Enter a value in the Size category for the number of lines deep you want the cap to be. Click on OK and the program will automatically change the letter to a point size appropriate for that number of lines.

Tables, coupons, price lists, numbered lists, and bulleted lists utilize indents and tabs. You should know the difference between decimal, centered, left- and right-aligned tabs, and know how to use tab leaders. When you can work confidently with the Tabs menu, you are well on your way to becoming a QuarkXPress expert.

The Tabs ruler

To affect the tab settings for any paragraph, you must first select the text and use the Text tool. Because tabs work on a full paragraph, it is not necessary that you select all the words, only that you locate the cursor in the paragraph somewhere. Once you identify the paragraph with the cursor, open the Tabs ruler by typing Command+Shift+T, or by selecting Tabs from the Style menu.

Copying tab specs

To apply the correct tab specs from one paragraph to the following paragraph, use the Text tool to select a line with the proper tab settings; drag down through the text to select the text to which you want to apply the preceding specs. Type Command+Shift+T, or select Tabs from the Style menu. As soon as the ruler opens, click OK. The correct tabs will be applied to the new text.

To add a tab simply select the type of tab that you currently need, then click on the ruler in the appropriate place or type in your measurement if you know exactly where you want it placed.

Creating hanging indents

You can see hanging bullets throughout this book where small squares precede text indented along its left margin. Working with the tab ruler to perform this function can be tricky. To make hanging indents, use the following steps:

1. Use the Text tool to select the paragraph where you want to apply the hanging indents.

2. Set the left indent and the amount of outdent for the first line of text, under the Formats menu. Normally if you have the left indent set to 2 picas the outdent for the first line is at -2 picas, taking it back to the normal left margin.

3. Next, with the text still selected, you need to choose the Tabs option under the Style menu. It is here where you define the placement for the tabs and choose whether the tab(s) should be left, right, centered, or decimal aligned. Continuing the sample above, you should set a left tab at 1p6 and a right tab at 2p0. Below is an example. Setting the first tab at 1p6 offers enough space for double digits within a numbered list to be right aligned.

4. Click on the OK button.

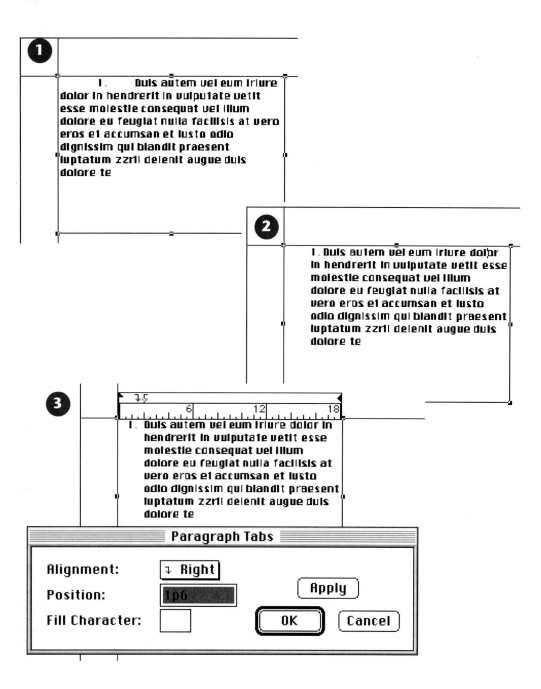

Creating coupons

You can find coupons in all types of documents—from flyers to brochures. If created skillfully, they can add to the professional appearance of the publication. Use the following guidelines when designing them:

- If you include a coupon in a document, it should be easy to fill out. Don't waste space with large type for the name, address, or city labels. These can be set in a small point size and remain perfectly readable—because readers have an expectation of what the labels will say.

- If you want respondents to include their area code with phone numbers, indicate that in "shorthand" by placing parentheses as part of the line.

- You can use dotted lines to separate the coupon from the rest of the copy on the page, or you can use a less traditional means for setting them off, as you see here.

- It is helpful to have a lead-in line to a coupon, something like, "Yes! I would love to receive a free copy of...." In such a case, make the Yes large and stylish.

- Pay attention to where you place a coupon. If the reader cuts it out, the page behind it is destroyed. If the reader is to keep the document, make sure what's lost behind the coupon is not something important.

- Many desktop-published documents use the Zapf Dingbat letter q when check boxes are needed. While this drop-shadowed box can be an appropriate choice, in most instances a checkbox without the drop shadow is a simpler and more elegant solution. You can create the checkbox by typing the solid Zapf Dingbat letter n, selecting it, and choosing the Outline style.

On the left is the Zapf Dingbat letter n with the outline style. On the right is the more commonly-used Zapf Dingbat letter q—a desktop publishing cliché.

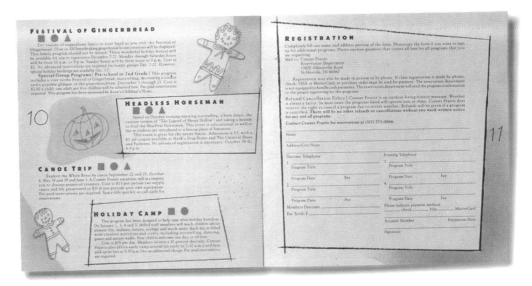

The example above shows an effective coupon that does not rely on the traditional dotted line. Designers: Laura Lacy-Sholly & James Sholly Antenna, Indianapolis Client: Conner Prairie

Creating coupons with tabs

You can create a quick and versatile coupon using tab settings and leaders to create the lines. The best aspect of this technique is that the coupon is a unified text block, and doesn't require the tiresome measuring required when using the Line tool. Here is how it works:

1. Type the information you want filled out in the coupon, and type a tab after each category (such as Name, Address, etc). Enter a return following the tab each time you want a new line.

2. Select all the text where lines are needed.

3. Choose Tabs under the Style menu.

4. Place a right tab at the end of the line by selecting right tab and clicking the cursor in the desired position on the tab ruler.

5. Select the leader style desired—in this case, a solid line. To create a solid line you press Shift+_. For leader dots you use a period (.).

6. For lines with more than one category (such as City, State, Zip in this example), select the line separately (triple-clicking selects an entire line) and place a tab stop in each location desired.

7. Experiment with the tab locations to get the right amount of distance between categories.

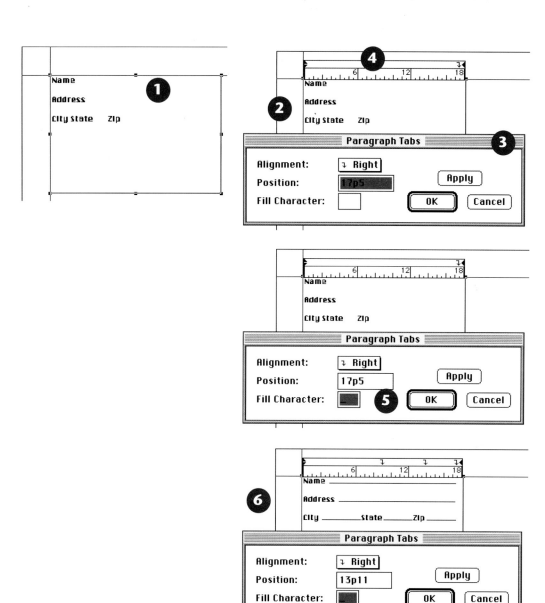

Numbered lists

There are some special considerations for the treatment of numbered lists:

■ If you have a numbered list with more than nine entries, make sure that the position for the numbers is set with a right aligned tab rather than left aligned. This is because the first digit in two-digit numbers needs to move out to the left.

■ It is very effective to treat the numbers like drop caps—especially if there are not many items in the numbered list. (If the publication is informal enough to do so.) Second color adds a nice touch. (See top right example.)

■ Numbers also can be used like headlines, centered above lines of text below the numbers. (See far right example.)

■ There is no limit to how many points can be in a numbered list. If you have more than 12, don't use a design element that will become too repetitive and tiring.

1 Lorem ipsum dolor sit amet, consectetuer adipiscing elit, sed diam non ummy nibh euismod tincidunt. Ut laoreet dolore magna aliquam erat volutpat.

2 Ut wisi enim as minim veniam, quis nostrud exerci. Tation ullamcorper suscipit lobortis nisl ut aliquip ex ea commodo consequat.

3 Hendrerit in vulputate velit esse molestie consequat, vel illum dolore eu feugiat nulla facilisis.

1

Lorem ipsum dolor sit amet, consectetuer adipiscing elit, sed diam non ummy nibh euismod tincidunt. Ut laoreet dolore magna aliquam erat volutpat.

2

Ut wisi enim as minim veniam, quis nostrud exerci. Tation ullamcorper suscipit lobortis nisl ut aliquip ex ea commodo consequat.

3

Hendrerit in vulputate velit esse molestie consequat, vel illum dolore eu feugiat nulla facilisis.

Bulleted lists

Bullet points are effective when handled correctly—and tiresome if treated in a clumsy or sloppy fashion. Although they seem simple, there are important considerations to remember when using them:

■ Balance the bullet size to the text. You want neither undersized or overpowering bullets. Option-8 in most fonts gives you a nice, round bullet.

■ Zapf Dingbats make interesting bullets. Consider squares (as you see here), triangles, or other geometric forms. Checkmarks, arrows, and similar bullets, although sometimes interesting, can become boring if overused.

■ If you have too many bullet points, the reader becomes distracted. With more than ten points, it's better to treat the bullets as a numbered list, if appropriate, or integrate the points into the body of text.

■ Never use only one or two bullet points. Bullets can look misplaced unless there are at least three separate ideas.

■ Hanging bullets are very effective in setting off points. The second and all succeeding lines of text fall under the indent of the first line; the bullet "hangs" out beyond the text. (Like it does here.)

■ If you are using two colors, consider printing the bullet in the second color.

Pull-quotes, like headlines and initial caps, provide another point of entry for the reader. Think of how many times you have skimmed through a magazine or other publication, and read a pull quote that literally pulled you into the entire article.

You can use pull quotes to break up an otherwise monotonous text-heavy page, or they can be used to entice the reader. Regardless of the reason, the designer must be careful when creating them not to change the role of the editor. What you choose to emphasize on a page can change the intent of the author. This is not a decision to be taken lightly.

There are many ways to design pull quotes. Here's one of them:

1. Select the text from body copy that you want to use as a pull quote and copy it to the clipboard (Command-C).

2. Off the edge of the page, draw the approximate size of the pull quote's text block (dragging with the mouse button held down.)

3. Release the mouse button and paste the copied text into the newly-described text block (Command-V).

This annual report makes extensive use of pull quotes as points of entry to draw the reader in. Designer: Deborah Reinerio, Red Hot Designs, San Francisco Client: O'Connor Hospital Foundation

4. Select all the text (Command-A).

5. Choose Character from the Style menu and select the new font, point size, alignment, color, and other specifications for the pull quote.

6. Using the Pointer tool, click on the text block for the pull quote and drag it over the body text. Measure, align, and adjust the text block until it is in the right position.

7. While you still have the text box selected, choose Runaround... from the Item menu, and specify the amount and style of text wrap. This will result in the body text flowing around the text box.

Typographer's quotation marks

Proper typographer's quotation marks and apostrophes are one of the small details which can make a project look professional. You can get them several different ways:

1. For opening quotes, type Option-[; for closing quotes, type Shift-Option-[.

2. For opening single quote, type Option-]; for closing single quote or apostrophe, type Shift-Option-].

The final way is to check the Convert quotes box when you place text that was written in a word-processing program.

Never use "inch marks" to put text in "quotes!"

Rules and underlines

Text that is laid out well will organize itself visually. Sometimes lines, or rules, are necessary to add structure and order to a page. When you use rules with finesse, they can add grace and elegance to a publication.

When using rules as part of a page design, consider the following:

- Restrict your palette of rules to one or two different styles.

- Consider printing the rules in a second color. If you're printing in black only, you could make rules a gray screen.

- If you are using a rule structure on one page of a publication, you should keep it consistent throughout the document. Set rules on the master pages.

- Rules used to lead from captions to a graphic should be handled so they are not confused with column rules. Use a different weight or color for them.

- Think of rules that are not strictly rules: rectangles, dotted lines (of any size), or lines made of leader.

Rules made of tab leader

Rules can be created by using tab leader. (You may want to refer to Tabs for further understanding on page 99.) You can create Tab leader rules using the following steps:

1. Measure the height for the dotted-line rules.

2. With the Text tool, create a new text block the same width as the height you've just measured. Create the approximate width with the mouse button held down as you drag. When you release the button, you will have a flashing cursor in the text box.

3. Type x-Tab-x-Return and open Tabs in the Style menu.

4. Place a right-hand tab at the end of the line. While you have it selected enter a letter, number, or dingbat character to use as the leader. Change the font, style, and size of this character by selecting the text block in the type tool and choosing Type specs.

5. Remove the x from the beginning and end of the line.

6. Using the Pointer tool, select the text block and choose text rotation. Place the rotated text block in the correct location inside a column guide.

7. Copy the text block, Step and repeat the copy on top of the original; hold the Shift key and move the copy to the next location.

Setting the weight of rules

You can now specify Rule widths from 0 to 504 points.

1. With a line selected, use the measurements palette to select the style of line you would like to choose.

2. Choose the style of line you want to use.

3. Type in a value for Line weight.

4. Hit the Return or Tab button.

Automatic rules

You can set Rules to automatically print a specified distance above or below type.

Horizontal rules

Thin rules often are used between columns of text to delineate them. Another use—more interesting because it is seen less—is to use thick horizontal rules above or below stories. Utilize color if you have that option. If your job is one color, they can be screened gray. If full-strength black, they may be too distracting. Also, if you are using horizontal rules, you probably should not use vertical rules. You can get too much of a good thing.

Reverse rules

The capability to make reverse rules means that you can place the rules on a solid color background. If you use this technique, don't make the reverse rule too thin or it will fill in during printing. A width of one point is safe—anything less is risky.

Intersecting rules

Care must be taken to measure rules perfectly where they intersect. It looks bad to have rules that meet improperly. Here again, 200% or 400% page view will allow for precise measurement.

Using rules with type

It is rarely acceptable to use the underline feature found under Character style, because the lines are drawn beneath the type without regard to descenders, commas, or spaces—with no control over color, placement, line weight, or other stylistic considerations. Underlining is simply an old typewriter convention that was used to indicate italics before it was possible to type italics. Now that we have the capability to do real type-setting, you should use italics wherever body copy is underlined. If someone has supplied text that contains underlining, the steps below describe how to use the Find/Change option under the Edit menu to change all the underlines to italics:

1. Click on the text block with either the Pointer tool or the Text tool.

2. Choose Find/Change (under the Edit menu), and deselect Ignore Attributes.

3. Under Find, select Underline within the Style options.

4. Under Change, choose Italic within the style menu.

5. Click on the Find Next button. You can also hold down the Option key to change the Find Next button to read Find First. This option works best. Once the first is found you can then click on Change All.

Styles

Another brilliant feature of QuarkXPress is the styles palette. With it, you can achieve great speed and accuracy when creating layouts. If you need to make a global change to a recurring element, it can be done with a few keystrokes.

Style definition

A style is a set of specifications that you can apply to a paragraph—a block of text that ends when you press a return—that formats the text for font, point size, leading, indents, tabs, and paragraph specifications.

Creating styles

Styles are easily created. You begin with the simple Style sheets… command found under the Edit menu. When the dialog box opens, you can select any category, such as Body text, and choose Edit. You'll see a submenu that allows you to change the specifications for Type, Formats, Tabs, or Rules. You'll recognize the dialog boxes for each of these, because they are the same as those found under the menus of the same name.)

It is also possible to create a new style based on an existing paragraph. Here's how it's done:

1. Place the text cursor in the paragraph that will be the basis for your new style.

2. Open the Styles Sheets… dialog box from the Edit menu.

3. Click on New.

4. Input all of the necessary information for Formats, Character, Rules, and Tabs.

5. Click Save, and the specifications of your paragraph will overwrite the previous specifications for that style.

Copying styles

When you want to copy a style sheet from another publication, click on Append... in the Style Sheets dialog box and locate the publication that you want to copy from. This will globally copy the entire style sheet from the publication; it is not possible to copy individual styles.

Importing styles

When importing word processed text from a program that does not support style sheets, you can identify individual styles by typing a style-name tag in front of each paragraph where a style change is to take place. You must have pre-defined these styles in your QuarkXPress file before importing the text. (To find out more about this, see page 87.)

Applying styles

Once you have defined styles, it is simple to apply them to any paragraph or group of paragraphs. In either Edit or Layout view, place the text cursor in a paragraph, or select a group of paragraphs, and click on the desired style in the Style Sheet palette.

Another quick way to assign styles is to place the cursor in your text, and pull down the Style menu to Style Sheets, drag through the submenu and release on the style you want to assign.

If you have a long word-processed document that will contain many different styles after placement in QuarkXPress, you may want to begin by applying one style, (Body text) to the entire document. Next, go back and reassign the appropriate headline, subhead, caption and other styles on a line-by-line basis to the document.

You may find it frustrating that you cannot assign more than one style to an individual paragraph, (for instance a Zapf Dingbat bullet point followed by a Stone Sans subhead). In this case, set the style for the text, set a placeholder letter for the bullet, and go through later and paste a copied dingbat over that letter.

If you apply a style to a paragraph that you've already formatted with bold, italic, etcetera, hold the Shift key when assigning the style and the locally placed formatting will not be dropped.

Editing styles

You've laid out the entire publication and discovered that there's too much text to fit it all in using 12 point type. It's very simple to open the Style Sheets... menu and edit Body text to a smaller point size, or to reduce the leading, change the tracking. Simply select the style name you want to change, click on Edit and change its specifications. It will take a moment or two for all the text in your document to recompose.

A very quick method for editing styles is to hold down the Command key and click on the style name in the style palette you want to edit. You will immediately see the editing dialog box.

Features such as spell checking, search and replace, and other text handling capabilities are a must for the expert user of QuarkXPress.

Below is an example of the capabilities that Quark offers the expert and novice user.

■ Find

If you don't know where a particular word or paragraph is in your document, you can choose the word, or an attribute you know is in the paragraph and go to the right place in the Find/Change dialog box. Quark will automatically take you to where it is located within your document and highlight the word.

■ Find by attribute

The capability to search by attribute is extremely useful. You can use it to restrict QuarkXPress's search actions to text with a specific format or combination of formats. Here is how it works:

1. Select from the Edit menu.

2. Deselect Ignore Attributes... to go to the next dialog box where you can specify which attributes (such as a particular font, bold or italic words, etcetera) to find.

3. Choose any attribute or combination of attributes for the search.

4. Click on the Find Next button or hold down the Option button to change the Find Next button to Find First.

```
┌──────────────────── Find/Change ────────────────────┐
│          Find what:              Change to:          │
│  ┌─☐ Text──────────┐      ┌─☐ Text──────────┐        │
│  │                 │      │                 │        │
│  │                 │      │                 │        │
│  └─────────────────┘      └─────────────────┘        │
│  ┌─⊠ Font──┐ ┌─⊠ Size─┐   ┌─⊠ Font──┐ ┌─⊠ Size─┐      │
│  │Helvetica│ │ 12 pt  │   │Helvetica│ │ 12 pt  │      │
│  └─────────┘ └────────┘   └─────────┘ └────────┘      │
│  ┌─⊠ Style────────────┐   ┌─⊠ Style────────────┐      │
│  │⊠ Plain  ☐ Underline│   │⊠ Plain  ☐ Underline│      │
│  │☐ Bold   ☐ Word u.l.│   │☐ Bold   ☐ Word u.l.│      │
│  │☐ Italic ☐ Small Caps│  │☐ Italic ☐ Small Caps│     │
│  │☐ Outline ☐ All Caps│   │☐ Outline ☐ All Caps│      │
│  │☐ Shadow ☐ Superscript│ │☐ Shadow ☐ Superscript│    │
│  │☐ Strike Thru ☐ Subscript│ │☐ Strike Thru ☐ Subscript│ │
│  └────────────────────┘   └────────────────────┘      │
│  ☐ Document  ☐ Whole Word  ⊠ Ignore Case  ☐ Ignore Attributes │
│  [ Find Next ]  [ Change, then Find ]  [ Change ]  [ Change All ] │
└──────────────────────────────────────────────────────┘
```

Change

Change is a more powerful find. Here are some changes you should perform on text routinely:

- Search for double spaces and replace them with single spaces. Many diehard typists insist that two spaces are needed to separate sentences in text, and in typing class, that was true. Typesetters always place just one space between a period and the sentence following it. To do otherwise leads to what are known as "rivers" of text. (This condition is aggravated when text is justified.) You may need to search two or three times, depending on the quality of the original word-processed text. Some keyboarders will place three or four spaces to create indents, or when creating charts place extra spaces to put text into columns. Replacing double spaces with single spaces may still leave double spaces after a first check.

- Search for space-period, and replace with period space; also search for space-comma, and replace with comma space.

- You also may need to search for space-dash-space, and replace with em or en-dashes.

- You can use Attributes to change fonts. For instance, to change all occurrences of Times Roman to Helvetica.

Spelling

Spell checking is not a substitute for proofreading, but rather augments it. Clearly, a spell checker would not alert you to "now" as a misspelled word. How would it know that you really meant "know"? Spell checking also functions well as a double check against words typed without a space between them, or to check the spelling of unfamiliar words on the spot. Here is how you can perform a spellcheck:

1. Choose Check Spelling from the Utilities menu.

2. You have the option to spell check the current word, story, or document.

3. Whenever a misspelled word is found, QuarkXPress will suggest alternatives. If you see the correct word, double-click on it and it will replace the one in question.

Displaying paragraphs and tabs

In checking the small details that give documents that professional look, it is important that all columns and indents are set with tabs rather than spaces. To check this, you can ask for a display of returns and tabs under the Show Invisibilities option within the View menu. Returns will be indicated with ¶, and arrows will show tabs. You can quickly scan your story to determine if you have placed tab stops and returns appropriately.

Using arrow keys

The arrow keys on the Macintosh can be used to move your cursor rapidly through text. Once you are accustomed to using them, you can fly through text editing tasks with lightning speed. Here are a few tricks when using the arrow keys to move the cursor:

- Holding the Command key while pressing the right or left arrow key, moves you through a document a word at a time.

- Holding the Shift key while pressing the right or left arrow key, selects letters as you move through them.

- Holding the Shift and Command keys together, while pressing the right or left arrow key, selects one word one at a time.

One feature has remained constant through each version of QuarkXPress and that is the concept of linking text blocks. Once understood, the linking works very well—but it can be tricky.

Working with text blocks

Think of text blocks like graphics. Focus on the shape of text blocks rather than what they contain. Move and resize text blocks using the Pointer tool.

There are two basic ways to alter text blocks: with the Text tool and with the Pointer tool. With the Text tool, you can edit text, change the font, point size, width, or other characteristics of the type inside a text block. With the Pointer tool, you can flow text into columns, change the width of columns, or force text into another column, or onto another page.

Consider these tips when manipulating text blocks:

- If you have measured the vertical alignment of a text block already, but want to change its column width, use the bottom handles. This keeps the vertical placement unchanged.

- It is sometimes necessary to combine two text blocks into one. This is easy to do. Click into the text block with the Text tool, and Select all (Command-A). Cut what you have selected (Command-X). Click an insertion point into the other text block, and paste (Command-V). The text you cut now flows into the remaining text block.

Find overset text

Overset text refers to text that have not been pulled down completely. A small box within the lower right corner of your text box indicates that you have text that is not being shown or used. This is a surefire way to ensure that you will never again suffer the embarrassment of a column whose last two lines have disappeared because a new line was typed before it.

To link text blocks follow the steps outlined below:

1. First select the Linking tool from the Tool palette. Hold down the Option key when selecting the tool, this will enable you to link multiple text blocks without having the linking tool revert back to the Hand tool after linking your first text block.

2. Select the starting point from which you want to begin linking. This will put a marque around the text block to show that it has been highlighted.

3. Next select the text block that you want to link. Continuing on until all text blocks have been linked. Note the arrows showing you the direction in which text blocks have been linked. This will help keep you from having to remember which text block is linked to another.

Hyphenation

Hyphenation is one of those important details that make for a quality document. Understanding the subtleties of hyphenation is very important; fortunately, QuarkXPress can help if you know where to look.

After you lay out the text in columns and edit for the final time, scan the columns for bad hyphenation. Words that break in funny places, large gaps, too many hyphens in a row—all these are hyphenations that you should change. Here are a few guidelines:

- Avoid leaving a widow or orphan—a single word or part of a word—on a line by itself. To make a premature or abrupt ending to the line above the widow, insert the cursor in front of the word and type Shift-Return to move another word down to the last line. This is a soft return that moves the entire word to the next line without activating other paragraph attributes such as indents and line spacing.

  Another solution may be selecting words in the last two lines of your paragraph and tightening the tracking to get the last syllable(s) into the preceding line.

- Three consecutive lines with hyphens is too many, and if more than a third of all lines in a paragraph are hyphenated, that's too many as well. Solutions may include the discretionary hyphen (Command-hyphen) just before the first character of a word you do not want hyphenated); increasing or decreasing the tracking on words or groups of words; changing the hyphenation zone; or changing the hyphenation in a paragraph from automatic to manual and hyphenating words individually when it appears appropriate to do so. Manual hyphenation can be selected by following these steps:

1. Select the paragraph or paragraphs where you want to change hyphenation.

2. Open the Hyphenation submenu (H&J) under the Edit menu.

3. To change the hyphenation zone, type in a new value. If you choose a larger value, more words will hyphenate—a smaller value allows fewer words to hyphenate.

4. To hyphenate any word, choose Auto Hyphenation and click on the OK button. In layout view, scan the right side of your columns at 200% view and wherever you want a word to hyphenate (from a line to the line above it), place your cursor in the word that you want to hyphenate and hold down the Command key and the Hyphen key.

In the Edit Hyphenation & Justification dialog box, you can choose to turn hyphenation on or off, make it a manual option, limit the number of consecutive hyphens, or change the hyphenation zone.

Cleaning up the rag

Rag refers to the unevenness of lines when text is left or right aligned. Some unevenness is desirable, but too much can be distracting. In this area attention to detail pays off with a subtle, but important impact on the overall appearance of your publication.

Clean up the rag by scanning the right side of each column and placing soft returns (hold down the Shift and Return keys) in front of small words that extend out too far. You also can use discretionary hyphens where you want words to move to the next line. Clean up rag at 200% view, moving down the page by holding down the Option key and the mouse button while dragging through the columns. The examples to the right illustrate how repositioning a small word at the end of line 3 (in the left paragraph) achieve a smoother look (see the right paragraph).

Three consecutive lines with hyphens is too many, and if more than a third of all lines in a paragraph are hyphenated, that's too many as well. Solutions may include increasing or decreasing the tracking on words or groups of words; changing the hyphenation zone, or changing the hyphenation in a paragraph from automatic to manual and hyphenating words individually when it appears appropriate to do so.

Three consecutive lines with hyphens is too many, and if more than a third of all lines in a paragraph are hyphenated, that's too many as well. Solutions may include increasing or decreasing the tracking on words or groups of words; changing the hyphenation zone, or changing the hyphenation in a paragraph from automatic to manual and hyphenating words individually when it appears appropriate to do so.

Graphics are essential for making a page design memorable. They can be used purely for decorative purposes, or they can convey information to the reader. The best graphics accomplish both.

The capability to juxtapose graphics and text sets QuarkXPress apart from all the word processing software that preceded it—and created a whole new discipline: desktop publishing. QuarkXPress's graphics handling has come a long way since 1985.

The photograph on this calendar looks at familiar objects in a new way—a great technique can create effective graphics.
Designer: Jennifer Morla, San Francisco
Client: American President Companies

Finding quality graphics for your publication is one of the primary challenges you face when using QuarkXPress. Rarely does even the best designer create all the graphics used in a document. Illustrations, photographs, charts, diagrams, and other graphics often come from many different sources.

Combining graphics with text is one of the primary functions of QuarkXPress. However, the program is not designed for creating graphics other than simple boxes, backgrounds, rules, or the like. The best graphics are scanned, drawn in other programs such as Aldus FreeHand or Adobe Illustrator, and then placed, resized, rotated, lightened, or otherwise adjusted as needed in QuarkXPress. Sometimes taking the conventional approach and having graphics physically pasted into artwork or stripped into film by your printer rather than as electronic files is the best choice. This is especially true for photographs.

Incorporating graphics into a design should not be an afterthought. If you find yourself searching for last-minute clip art to make a page prettier, you're probably on the wrong track. It's much better to lay out a page with the graphics in mind when you begin.

There are numerous sources for graphic enhancements to your pages, depending on your budget, talent, time frame and imagination. Let's look at some of them.

Photography

Photography is a common source for graphics. Photographs lend immediacy to a topic, and tell a story with a level of accuracy that illustrations seldom match.

■ Stock photos

Numerous companies publish catalogs containing photographs which can be purchased. They offer thousands of images, arranged by category, and just looking through the catalogs can ignite your imagination. Some stock catalog companies are now offering photos on CD-ROM, that can be searched by keywords, subjects, artist, and so forth. You can use scanned photos from a catalog to create comps for selling your client on a particular image, or use low-resolution versions off a CD. The stock company will send you the original or high-resolution file by overnight delivery if you decide to purchase the photo rights.

It is never permissible to use scans of stock photographs for final reproduction on any kind of publication, regardless of how much a scan has been altered or distorted. This is a violation of the copyright law.

Some stock photo companies that offer catalogs are:

Allstock
(206) 282-8116

Peter Arnold, Inc.
(800) 289-7468

Bettman
(212) 777-6200

Comstock
(800) 225-2727

Leo de Wys, Inc.
(800) 284-3399

FPG International
(212) 777-4210

Ibid, Inc.
(312) 733-8000

The Image Bank
(212) 529-6700

Photovault
(415) 552-9682

The Stock Market
(800) 999-0800

Third Coast Stock
(800) 323-9337

Vintage Images
(703) 207-9888

Westlight
(800) 872-7872

Sources

■ Commissioned photos

Many photographers specialize. Some only work in studios, others do portraits on location. Some photograph food exclusively, others architecture. Styles vary markedly, and you should always see a portfolio of a photographer's work before you contract to work with one.

It can be rewarding to work with a professional photographer—and hard work too—to get exactly the right photographs for your publication. You must be well prepared and use the photographer's time well. Have a clear idea what you want in terms of color, lighting conditions, subjects, and other variables before you arrange the photography shoot. To have to do a reshoot is expensive—and causes delays.

■ Photo CD

Kodak Photo CD technology has made it even easier to incorporate photos into a publication. You can take any group of slides, (or soon, 4" x 5" transparencies), and have them placed on a Photo CD when the film is developed, or if you cannot yet locate such a service, send them out to a service bureau for scanning and placement onto a Photo CD.

You can import Photo CD images into QuarkXPress. Of course, you need a compatible CD drive to access the images and specific and inexpensive software (such as Aldus Fetch or Kodak's Access) to be able to view, retrieve, and convert Photo CD images into a file format acceptable to QuarkXPress. Low-resolution images can be placed in your document for a quicker working file and faster proof printing. Later, when the file is being sent for final output, the images can be replaced with their high-resolution counterparts. To import images directly from Photo CD, follow these steps:

1. Choose Get Picture from the File menu.

2. Locate the Photo CD, select Overview, PCD file, and click on the OK button.

3. In the Photo CD filter v.1.0 dialog box, specify color format and resolution desired.

4. Click OK to place the file.

5. Click to place the image on the page.

■ Non-professional photos

Often, a designer is called upon to work with existing photographs. This can be a challenge because the photos supplied by a client may be of varied quality. Photos of different people featured in the same article might be different sizes, have different backgrounds, lighting conditions, and so forth. The best design solution in this case might be to scatter the photos throughout the article so they don't invite comparison. They should all be the same size (unless one person is more important to the story than the others), and should be cropped appropriately to eliminate distracting backgrounds.

■ Photo retouching

Photo retouching used to be an expensive process only performed by professionals before the advent of electronic publishing technology. Now, with Adobe Photoshop, Image Studio, or PixelPaint Professional, you can change backgrounds, montage images, do color correction, blur, sharpen, take out troublesome details, and perform many other manipulations. This can result in humorous juxtapositions, dramatic combinations, or just simply improvement of a questionable photo.

Commissioned art

Like photographers, every city has illustrators who specialize in different subjects, techniques and media. In developing illustrations for your publication, some may require a lot of direction to produce what you want, while others will be able to grasp your idea immediately and come up with a terrific solution. In either case, you should see rough sketches first, before an illustration is completely developed. When assigning illustrations, it is important to specify the intended proportions, size and placement of the illustration on the page.

Clip art

Clip art refers to ready-made illustrations, either as hard copy or on disk, that you can add to publications. There is a lot of useful clip art available. Quality varies widely, and a lot of images are seen repeatedly in print. One reliable source is any of the excellent Dover books or disks of copyright-free art. Dover can be reached at (516) 294-7000.

Both the woman and the wall she is sitting on are copyright-free clip art from Dover.

The dramatic "Thank You" script on the left was provided by a calligrapher, scanned, and traced in Adobe Illustrator, and imported into Quark as an EPS file. It was then foil stamped when the piece was printed.
Designer/Calligrapher: Deborah Reinerio, Red Hot Designs, San Francisco
Client: Mills-Peninsula Hospital foundation

Video images

If your Macintosh is properly configured with a video capture card and associated software, you can take still frame "grabs" from VCRs, camcorders, broadcast or cable television, or from a still video camera for use as graphics. (If you use grabs from commercial sources for publication, you may be infringing on copyright laws.) Most video sources are analog—data as a continually fluctuating voltage rather than discrete pieces of information—and the frame grabber serves to convert them into a digital format like other Macintosh graphics.

Most frame grabbers either save a PICT image or have an acquire or plug-in module for Adobe PhotoShop so that images can be captured directly into that application. From PhotoShop you can save the image in the PICT or TIFF format for placement into QuarkXPress. While video is an inherently low-resolution source, displaying the scanned lines of which the image is made, it can produce acceptable quality. Reducing a video image to 50% of its original size or running a low-level blur on it in PhotoShop can help to hide these artifacts.

Portrait of Jackson
©1988 Michael Nolan
This image was originally a video scan capturing a live subject through the MacVision video interface. Here, a laser print was scanned and saved as a TIFF file. The scan was then lightened with the style palette... and the magenta image was changed to black and white, which is why it appears to be transparent. Each scan was assigned a color in the color palette.

Screen captures

When you are in any program on the Macintosh, you can take a snapshot of whatever the screen is displaying. This screen capture can be imported into QuarkXPress for use as a graphic, whether in black and white or color. (Many of the figures in this book are screen captures.)

If you have a color monitor and do not have graphics software, you can change the desktop pattern on your screen display and then make a capture of the pattern and place it into QuarkXPress like the figures on this page. To change the desktop pattern display, open the Control Panels and General Controls. You can change individual pixels by picking a new color from the palette along the bottom and clicking on the display on the left, or use preset patterns by clicking on the small arrows above the display on the right to scroll through the choices. When finished, click on the screen displayed and your desktop pattern will change to the one you have selected.

The resolution of screen captures is that of your screen, usually 72 DPI (dots per inch). If you intend to use the image smaller than captured, or desire a pixellated look, you will find the resolution satisfactory for a graphic background.

This is a simple graphic obtained by making a screen capture of a monitor's background, importing it into QuarkXPress, cropped and enlarged.

Here is how to make and use a screen capture:

1. Make sure that the screen is displaying exactly what you wish to capture, and that the pointer is not in the picture, unless you want it to be.

2. Even if you are holding down the mouse button to display a menu, type Command-Shift-3. A PICT screen capture is saved.

3. Use QuarkXPress's Get Picture command under the File menu to place the graphic into your publication. It will be found on the main level of your hard drive, with the name Picture 1, Picture 2, and so on.

4. After the screen capture has been placed, it can be sized, cropped, rotated, or otherwise transformed in QuarkXPress.

This is the same screen capture as shown below left, resized, and uncropped.

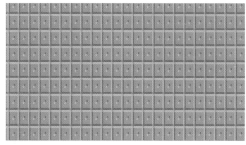

Again, this is the same screen capture, cropped, stretched, and resized.

Conversion

To be used in QuarkXPress documents, graphics must be converted to electronic format. This can be done in several ways. They can be scanned, drawn in a graphics program, or traced and redrawn. This section will explore these different methods.

Scanning

There are many different types of scanners, ranging from small, hand-held units to large drum models. Their workings are similar to those of photocopiers, but the images they capture are translated into data files for electronic display and output.

As always, the type of publication you're producing will dictate which kind of scanner you employ for converting your graphics to electronic format. For a document reproduced from laser prints, it is not necessary to use a scanner with resolution higher than 300 SPI. (While it is common to use DPI to indicate the resolution of a scanner, it is not accurate. A scanner actually examines samples, not dots while it scans.)

Service bureaus often provide flatbed, slide/transparency and drum scanning services, though at a relatively high cost. (You can expect these costs to drop as low-cost Photo CD technology becomes more widely available.)

■ Handheld scanners

Handheld scanners are inexpensive, and great for capturing images to be used as templates for redrawing in Illustrator or FreeHand. Some have resolution as high as 400 SPI. and support 256 levels of gray. One problem with them is that you may have to combine separate images to create a full page.

■ Flatbed scanners

With these scanners you lay a piece of art—a photograph, drawing, or other image—directly on a glass, close the lid and scan. They can be either black and white or color, and their resolution ranges from 300 SPI. to 600 SPI. Black and white flatbed scanners support up to 256 levels of gray, completely acceptable for QuarkXPress projects.

One of my favorite things to do with flatbed scanners is scan 3-D objects. You can use anything—tools, hands, crumpled paper, flowers—and get some great scans with shadows and texture. You need to creatively drape the object to block light because the top probably won't close. Two cautions: be careful not to scratch the glass on the flatbed scanner; never look into a scanner to scan your face.

Slide/transparency scanners

If the photographs for your publication are provided to you as slides, you can have them scanned. Scanned slides produce a great image, as long as the slide scanner which is being used has been recently calibrated, and the operator is knowledgeable. Larger transparencies can also be scanned, and produce even better results because there can be higher resolution since the image is larger than a slide and allows the scan to contain more data.

Drum scanners

On these scanners, art is attached to a drum that rotates rapidly and scanned at very accurate, very high resolution. These scanners are found in service bureaus and prepress companies.

Scanning resolution

Resolution is determined in dots per inch, (DPI) and the higher your resolution, the sharper your image. When art is scanned, it must be at a DPI two times the intended line screen of the halftone. That means if you are going to print at a line screen of 133 (metal plates, mid- to high-quality printing) you will need scans at 266 DPI. Of course, this formula changes if you intend to reduce or enlarge the scan once it's placed on the page. If you'll be using it at 50% its original size, scan at 133 DPI for a 133 line screen. If you'll be using it at twice its size, you'll need a scan of 532 DPI. These are just guidelines. If you are unsure how large you'll be using a particular image, scan at higher resolution, and if you don't need it the only consequence is that the file will contain more information than it needs and will print more slowly.

The TIFF scan above is assigned 53 lines per inch form the style menu. The same scan below has been assigned 133 LPI screen.

Graphics software

Many different graphics programs can be used to produce, retouch, and prepare art for electronic publication in QuarkXPress. Each program serves specific purposes, and it is beyond the scope of this book to examine any of them in detail. They can be used alone or in conjunction with one another to produce graphics.

Once you have created a file in any of these programs, it can be saved in a format QuarkXPress can accept, import it into your publication. Color information assigned in the graphic program will be maintained in QuarkXPress and can be separated to film for process or spot color reproduction when the QuarkXPress file is output to film.

Some typical graphics programs that can be used with QuarkXPress (and there are others) are listed below:

- **Drawing**
  Aldus FreeHand
  Adobe Illustrator
  MacDraw Pro
  Corel Draw
  DeskDraw

- **3-D**
  Swivel 3-D
  RayDream Designer

- **Paint**
  PixelPaint
  Adobe Photoshop
  Fractal Painter
  Image Studio
  Color Studio
  SuperPaint
  Aldus Digital Darkroom

Scans for tracing

Often, a quick sketch of something is scanned, and imported for use as a template into Aldus FreeHand, Adobe Illustrator or a similar program to be traced. In object-oriented drawing programs like these you can achieve precise line weights, fills, and colors, that would require unusually well-developed drawing skills and the finest art tools if created by hand.

Once the tracing is completed, delete the scan itself, leaving the new drawing in the file. You should generally save the drawing as an Encapsulated PostScript (EPS) file. It then can be placed into a QuarkXPress document as a graphic.

Acceptable file formats

After creating work in graphics software for use in QuarkXPress, you must save your file in a format QuarkXPress can accept. Here are some recommendations for specific software programs:

Adobe Illustrator	EPS
Aldus FreeHand	EPS
Aldus Persuasion	PICT
Aldus TableEditor	PICT
Arts & Letters 3.01	EPS, TIFF
AutoCad 9.1	EPS
CorelDRAW!	EPS, TIFF
DXF	DXF
Encapsulated PostScript	EPS
Excel Charts	WMF, XLC
Excel Spreadsheets	XLS
Harvard Graphics	EPS
HPGraphicsGallery	TIFF
Lotus Freelance Graphics	EPS, TIFF
MacPaint	PNT
Micrografix Design	TIFF
PC Paintbrush	TIFF
Publishers Paintbrush	PCX
TIFF files	TIFF
Windows Metafile	WFF, WMF
Windows Paintbrush 3.0	BMP, PCX

Other supported graphic formats

BMP, DCS, PCX, PhotoCD(PCD), PNT, TIF, CMYK TIFF

This rate card uses a photograph of a distinctive brick wall from the client's building. The photograph was scanned, posterized, and lightened, to serve as a graphic pattern.
Designer: Mike Bertoni, PRINTZ Electronic Design, San Francisco
Client: Varitel Video

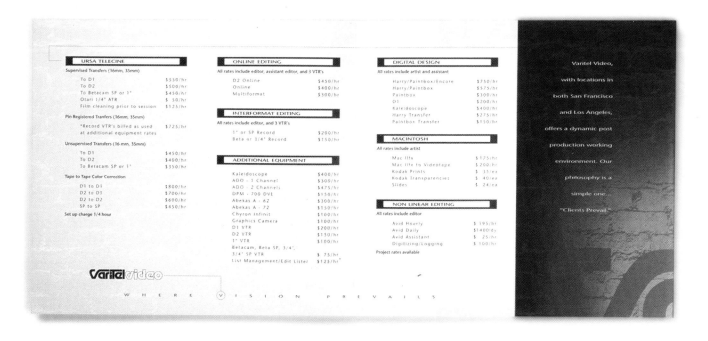

URSA TELECINE

Supervised Transfers (16mm, 35mm)

To D1	$550/hr
To D2	$500/hr
To Betacam SP or 1"	$450/hr
Otari 1/4" ATR	$ 50/hr
Film cleaning prior to session	$125/hr

Pin Registered Tranfers (16mm, 35mm)

*Record VTR's billed as used at additional equipment rates	$725/hr

Unsupervised Transfers (16 mm, 35mm)

To D1	$450/hr
To D2	$400/hr
To Betacam SP or 1"	$350/hr

Tape to Tape Color Correction

D1 to D1	$800/hr
D2 to D1	$700/hr
D2 to D2	$600/hr
SP to SP	$450/hr

Set up charge 1/4 hour

ONLINE EDITING

All rates include editor, assistant editor, and 3 VTR's

D2 Online	$450/hr
Online	$400/hr
Multiformat	$300/hr

INTERFORMAT EDITING

All rates include editor, and 3 VTR's

1" or SP Record	$200/hr
Beta or 3/4" Record	$150/hr

ADDITIONAL EQUIPMENT

Kaleidoscope	$400/hr
ADO - 1 Channel	$305/hr
ADO - 2 Channels	$475/hr
DPM - 700 DVE	$150/hr
Abekas A - 62	$300/hr
Abekas A - 72	$150/hr
Chyron Infinit	$100/hr
Graphics Camera	$100/hr
D1 VTR	$200/hr
D2 VTR	$150/hr
1" VTR	$100/hr
Betacam, Beta SP, 3/4", 3/4" SP VTR	$ 75/hr
List Management/Edit Lister	$125/hr

DIGITAL DESIGN

All rates include artist and assistant

Harry/Paintbox/Encore	$750/hr
Harry/Paintbox	$575/hr
Paintbox	$300/hr
D1	$200/hr
Kaleidoscope	$400/hr
Harry Transfer	$275/hr
Paintbox Transfer	$150/hr

MACINTOSH

All rates include artist

Mac IIfx	$175/hr
Mac IIfx to Videotape	$200/hr
Kodak Prints	$ 35/ea
Kodak Transparencies	$ 40/ea
Slides	$ 24/ea

NON LINEAR EDITING

All rates include editor

Avid Hourly	$ 195/hr
Avid Daily	$1400/dy
Avid Assistant	$ 25/hr
Digitizing/Logging	$ 100/hr

Project rates available

Varitel video

WHERE VISION PREVAILS

Varitel Video,

with locations in

both San Francisco

and Los Angeles,

offers a dynamic post

production working

environment. Our

philosophy is a

simple one.

"Clients Prevail."

After you have converted graphics to an electronic file format, they can be imported into QuarkXPress. There are different ways of doing this, and choices must be made based on how the graphic will be updated, and where the information it contains is stored.

Draw- and paint-type graphics

The graphics that QuarkXPress is able to import fall into two categories: Draw-type (object-oriented) graphics, and Paint-type (bitmapped) images. Draw-type images use mathematical equations to describe the paths of lines and fills; therefore, they can be re-sized once in QuarkXPress with no degradation of quality. Paint-type images, which are drawings done in paint programs or scans, are resolution-dependent and their quality can deteriorate as they are sized larger. Both draw- and paint-type graphics can be imported into QuarkXPress similarly.

Formats QuarkXPress imports

TIFF, BMP, PCX, EPS, MacPaint, WMF and PICT formats can all be imported by QuarkXPress.

If your graphics software can save a file in one of these formats, graphics you create can be used in QuarkXPress. If not, you may need a graphics conversion program to change your image into one of these formats. This may also be true if you wish to import a draw-type graphic created on a PC into QuarkXPress for the Macintosh. Some conversion programs include HotShot Graphics by SymSoft, HiJaak by Inset Systems, or The GraphicsLink Plus+ by Harvard Graphics.

Placing graphics

Placing graphics is done with QuarkXPress's Get Picture command, found under the File menu. This method of importing a graphic enables you to create a link to the original source file, meaning that the file information does not need to be included in your QuarkXPress document, and that the graphic can be updated automatically if the source file changes.

Pasting graphics

This method of importing graphics uses the Macintosh Clipboard. You can Copy the graphic with the source program open, then open your QuarkXPress document and paste.

Publish/subscribe

If you are using a Macintosh with System 7.0 or higher, you can use the Publish/subscribe method to import graphics. In this two step process, you first publish the graphic when you are in the source program by exporting it in a format QuarkXPress can use. Once in QuarkXPress, you then subscribe to that graphic by choosing Subscribe to... from the Editions submenu on the Edit menu, selecting the file which you wish to import, and clicking Subscribe. This is a good importing choice if you want to reuse a graphic in multiple applications, because you can update all the subscribers automatically.

External linking

When you import graphic files QuarkXPress will import a low-resolution version of the graphic for display purposes only, and establishes a link to the original graphic. You must be sure that this link is maintained for proper printed output. If not, the low-res display graphic will be substituted even with high resolution imagesetting.

Automatic link updating

When a graphic is placed, QuarkXPress establishes a link to the original document on your hard drive. QuarkXPress will automatically search for and update the file as long as the original is found. If the original file has been moved, Quark will display a dialog box letting you know that some or all graphics have either been moved or updated. To check on the current graphics and the current status of each you can access the Picture Usage dialog box from the Utilities menu. Once selected you will see the graphic name, location, file type, page number, and current status.

You can update the status of all or any graphic by double clicking on each. You will be prompted by a dialog box to locate the graphic and update its location. The name of the current file that you are looking for will always be displayed at the top of this dialog box for your reference. This comes in handy when you have to update multiple graphics at once.

Keep in mind that Quark will not be able to locate a file that has changed formats, for example a PICT file to an EPS file. This is because if the original was once a PICT Quark will search for PICT files only, thus not being able to locate the eps file. The only way to update the graphic is to replace it entirely within the picture box itself.

Library palette

This is an easy way to import and organize collections of frequently used text and graphics. You can categorize and search for objects by key words, display names, and thumbnail images.

Adding objects to the Library is easy. Select the object, open Library from the Utilities menu, and drag the selected object onto the palette. All link information about the object is retained and added to the Library.

Inline graphics

When you want a graphic to remain with specific text, it can be placed as an inline graphic. Inline graphics can be only used when the graphic will fit entirely within the flowed text block.

To import a graphic as part of a text block (or "inline"), place the cursor in the text where you wish to insert the graphic. Use the Place or Paste command, and the graphic will become part of the text block. You can also copy or cut an existing graphic from the page and paste it into the text.

It is not possible to flow several lines of text around an inline graphic; instead, when the graphic is imported, it becomes a "character" in a line and has auto leading characteristics based on its size. The graphic takes its spacing cues from the surrounding text. It's often necessary to adjust the leading or spacing of an inline graphic. Here's how to do it:

1. To adjust leading, select the paragraph which includes the graphic. Open the Leading... dialog box (Command+Shift+E) and change the leading to whatever value is being used for all the text in the text block.

2. To move the graphic vertically, use the Baseline Shift option within the Style menu. The graphic can then be moved up or down.

3. To adjust the distance from the graphic to text that precedes or follows it, place the cursor between the graphic and text and select the Formats Option from the Style menu. Add or deleting paragraph space both before and after.

The text block below shows a scan used twice as an inline graphic.

Lorem ipsum dolor sit amet, consectetuer adipiscing elit, sed diam nonummy nibh euismod tincidunt. Ut laoreet dolore magna aliquam erat volutpat.

Ut wisi enim ad minim veniam, quis nostrud ecerci. Tation ullamcorper suscipit lobortis pisl ut aliquip.

The leading of inline graphics can be tricky. On the left, you can see that the first line containing the graphic has different leading from the rest of the text block. This can be solved by selecting the entire text block, and specifying a leading value that can accommodate the size of the graphic

Finding, creating and importing the right graphics for your publication is just the beginning. You must make the most of your graphics when you place them onto the page. There are many ways to use graphics very effectively.

The photograph used on the cover of this brochure is featured prominently because it is so dramatic.
Design: The Newsletter Company, Campbell, CA
Client: Waernes Technology Corporation

Feature graphics prominently

If the graphic is very strong or colorful, or if it conveys vital information, it should be treated as a stand-alone element. Type should not be printed on top of the graphic, nor should the graphic be small. Instead, feature it prominently and consider a bleed off the page, placement across two pages, callouts or captions pointing to the graphic, or other methods of drawing attention to it.

Integrate graphics with text wrap

Text wrap is a good way to integrate a prominent graphic into a page. Here's how to work with QuarkXPress's text wrap feature:

1. Arrange the text on your page, and import the graphic by using the "Get Picture" command under File.

2. Place the graphic on top of the text which will wrap around it. While the graphic is selected, choose "Runaround..." from the Item menu.

3. You have four Wrap options from which to choose when the object is first placed: None, Item, Auto, and Manual. Choose Item to be able to adjust the amount of text wrap on the top, left, bottom, and right hand sides of the graphic box. Choose Auto to set the same amount of text wrap around an entire image. Choosing Manual will let you vary the amount of text wrap around all sides.

4. When you choose Manual your graphic is surrounded by a dotted line defining the area where text will not print. If you click and drag on one of these lines, it can be moved farther away from the graphic, or even inside the boundaries of the graphic (if you want text to print on the graphic). If you click once on a line and release the mouse button, you break the line and insert a new point in it. These points can be created and moved around to define how the text will wrap around the graphic.

5. Each time you change the boundaries of the wrap, the text in the affected story reflows. This can be cumbersome and time-consuming. If a lot of adjustment of the border must be done, it's best to hold down the Shift key while doing this. Holding down the Shift key will not let the screen redraw while you are inserting/adjusting points. When all points have been added or moved you can release the Shift key to let the text redraw.

6. Pay attention to how the type is affected by the text wrap. Don't allow several lines of narrow columns with just one-word in them. It's better not to use text wrap than to create ugly or difficult to read type just for the sake of a wrap. Resizing the graphic slightly by holding the Shift key and moving one of the graphic's handles (as opposed to the boundary's handles) changes the flow of the text.

Use graphics under text

If your photograph or image is not particularly strong on its own, it may look better placed under the text. Use caution when taking this approach, however, because text can be difficult to read with a strong or distracting graphic behind it. (This is a particular risk when you are printing in only one color.)

Use color whenever possible

If you are using a second color in your publication, you may wish to include that color in your graphics, even if they are originally black and white line art or grayscale images. Grayscale photographs and drawings have tonal variation. Your second color will appear in many different levels, giving added impact to the document.

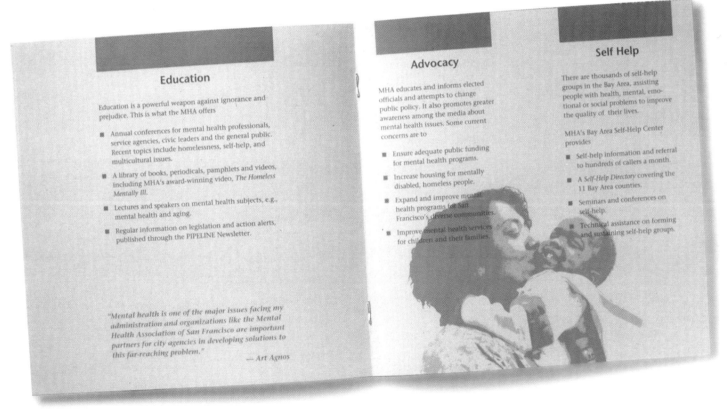

The graphic featured in this brochure is placed behind the text.
Designer: Michael J. Nolan
Client: San Francisco Mental Health Association

Backgrounds

Backgrounds are patterns, textures or other images that lie beneath the text and graphics of a page. They can add pleasing depth and interest to any printed piece.

Sources for backgrounds

There are many creative options for backgrounds. One designer I know took photographs of the concrete walls in a parking garage and then scanned them to create an effective background. I once used lace from a bridal veil with black paper behind it on a flatbed scanner to create a background for a wedding invitation. Sheets of wrapping paper, or even imported book papers found in art supply stores also make good sources for backgrounds.

Backgrounds can be created with a scanner, or drawn in a graphics or paint program.

The graphics shown here were made by scanning a doily and some dried flowers.

Background intensity

If scans are used as backgrounds with type placed over them, they should be carefully controlled so that they are not too strong; otherwise, the type is hard to read. If you are printing in one color, the background must be even more subdued. The Item menu offers features in QuarkXPress to let you lighten TIFF or PICT scans used as backgrounds. (See gradient fills, page 150). Because laser prints do not give an accurate indication of the darkness of a screen, you should run a paper imagesetter test to study the contrast between the background and the type overlaying it.

Sometimes backgrounds are a solid color, a screened color, or a gradation of color. It is important to judge how readable text will be in these situations as well. For proofing purposes, it is best to use a system such as an IRIS proofer, because a laser printer will not print accurate levels of contrast.

Other backgrounds

Even if you don't have access to a scanner or an illustration program, you can still create backgrounds for your documents. Use QuarkXPress's graphics tools to create rectangles, squares, circles, or ellipses, and overlay them with lines or other patterns found within the program. Or, take a more conventional route and have your printer strip in photographs or even photocopies that you provide. Because this will eliminate some control for you, be sure to see a blueline (a composite proof made from film negatives) and maybe even do a press check (examination of the first few printed pieces before the entire run is printed), to make sure that the background isn't too strong.

The brochure shown on the left uses a background pattern created in Adobe Illustrator, and saved as an EPS file. The letterhead on the right was created with TIFF scans placed over one another.
Designer: Carol Kappel, Pearson, Crahan & Fletcher, Indianapolis
Client: St. Vincent's Hospital

There are two kinds of backgrounds in the St. Vincent's Hospital material. The letterhead from the Breast Center uses scans, while the annual report contains PostScript patterns drawn in another program.

The following steps show how to create a page similar to the letterhead, using backgrounds of grayscale scans and spot color printing. (This applies only to TIFF or PICT format files, which can be lightened with QuarkXPress.)

1. Set up an 8 $^1/_2$" x 11" page with 0 margins on all sides. This will allow you to see the edge of the page when guidelines are displayed after the scans have been placed on it.

2. Make sure guidelines are set to Front in the Preferences dialog box so you can measure where to crop the image placed on top

3. Place the TIFF or PICT scan which serves as the bottom layer on your page by using the Get Picture command from the File menu.

4. Use the Pointer tool on one of the handles of the selected image and hold the Command+Option+Shift keys to restrain the proportions of the image as you drag and enlarge it to fill the page. The first scan placed must extend $^1/_4$" beyond the page on all sides.

5. Select the scan, copy it and place the copy exactly on top of the original.

6. Select the Style menu, and use the Other Contrast option to lighten the second scan enough for type to be readable over it. (You should run a test file on a high-resolution printer to make sure the lightness is correct.)

7. Use the Cropping tool on the corners and crop the top scan to measurement lines an equal distance in from the edge of the page on all sides. (You may wish to crop in a bit more from the bottom for better "framing".)

8. Place the type you'll be using on top of the lighter scan, and choose another color for it if you are printing two-color.

5   **6**

7

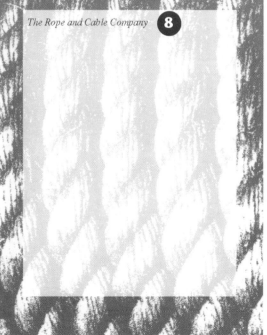

The Rope and Cable Company **8**

Borders

Borders are an effective way to frame a graphic, pull quote, photograph, or a full page—if they are used with restraint and purpose. A good border complements the message of the publication.

Use discretion when creating borders. Some users of QuarkXPress can fall prey to "border-mania," using combinations of drop shadows, double or triple rules, and rounded corner boxes, on the same page.

Here are some simple ideas for creating borders that avoid the cliches:

A drop shadow border

This drop shadow is soft and natural in its gradation. You may need to experiment a few times to get it right.

1. Create a rectangle, or rounded corner box, with a white fill.

2. Select the placeholder box and duplicate it by using the Step & Repeat option. Paste 9 of these 1 point down and 1 point over to the right.

3. Select the first copied figure, and change its fill to 90% screen. Send it to the back.

4. Continue with the succeeding figures, changing fills to the next lower screen value with each one, and send each one to the back. The bottom layer should have a 10% screen.

A line border

This simple border can be created in seconds. Additional layers in different colors give it even more interest.

1. Create two rectangles of different sizes, select a line pattern from the Fill menu for the larger one and give the smaller one paper fill.

2. Choose a second color from the color palette.

3. Place the smaller rectangle on top of the larger one using the "Bring to front" command from the Edit menu, and measure the distance from the edge on all sides to make sure it's correct. (Do this at 200% or 400% view, but don't try to count the lines for measurement because their number changes in each view).

A dingbat border

Explore the variety of Zapf Dingbats by choosing Key Caps from under the Apple menu, changing the font under the Key Caps menu, and pressing different combinations of the Shift and Option keys to see what different keystrokes yield from this versatile font. Then choose one or several dingbats to make a border such as this one:

1. Create a text block, and type into it the dingbat characters desired for the border.

2. Select the type, and use the "Justify…" command under Alignment.

3. Copy the text block and paste a new one over it.

4. While the pasted object is selected, using text rotation, rotate it 180° and move it down in place for the bottom border.

5. Create a text block of the appropriate length for the sides, adding the proper number of characters.

6. Copy that text block, paste it and rotate it using the Measurements palette or Rotation tool into the proper position for the other side.

7. Use the Box tool, and choose appropriate line weights and colors to surround the dingbats. View at 400% to make sure measurements are accurate.

Charts and Graphs

Charts and graphs are a very effective way to summarize numerical data and tell a visual story. They take many forms, from pie charts to bar graphs. Many spreadsheet programs have the capability to create graphics from the data that has been entered. If you have a program like this, it is efficient to build your chart or graph in the program and import into QuarkXPress.

Importing spreadsheets

There are several methods of getting charts and graphs into QuarkXPress, including Place, Paste link and Subscribe. Before styling your graphic in the spreadsheet program, be certain that you are using fonts and colors which will look good in your document, because once placed into your QuarkXPress publication, they can only be changed using the source program. You may wish to create headings or other labels in QuarkXPress, to have more immediate control over how they look in your publication.

When a chart or graph is imported from a spreadsheet program, it will be treated as a graphic, which means you can enlarge/reduce, crop, stretch, rotate or otherwise manipulate it.

Basic graphs created in QuarkXPress

If you do not have a spreadsheet program capable of building a chart or graph, you can use the graphics tools in QuarkXPress to do so. Here's a simple process for building a bar graph (the measurements are arbitrary; you can use your own):

1. Draw a one point horizontal line 3 inches long, and place an 8 point 0, right aligned, to the left of the line.

2. Copy the line and the text block next to it, and choose Step and Repeat from the Item menu. For the distance, choose .2 inches for vertical offset 0 for horizontal offset, and paste 10 copies. This will yield 11 lines, evenly spaced .2 inches apart.

3. Beginning with the second text block from the bottom, click into the block, choose Select All and retype 10. Do the same and enter 20 for the next one, 30 for the one after that, and so forth, until the top line is labeled 100.

4. Create a rectangle that is .2 inches wide, and extends from the 0 line to just above the 50 line. It should have a 20% fill and no lines.

5. Copy the rectangle and multiple paste it six times with a vertical offset measurement of .4 inch, and horizontal offset of 0.

6. Use the middle handle on the top of each rectangle to adjust its height. 35 percent would be midway between the 30 and 40 line. These adjustments will be by eye, and it should be fairly easy to make them look accurate.

7. You can "decorate" the graph any way you wish, but the basic principle should be to keep it simple.

Another way to create the same type of graph is to make the lines and labels one text block using tabs and leaders (see Tabs/Indents, page 96). This enables you to change the type specifications for everything at once. You can also use paragraph rules instead of leader tabs to have great control over line styles.

Simple graphs such as this one below, can be made quickly using Quark's Step and Repeat... feature by following the steps outlined here.

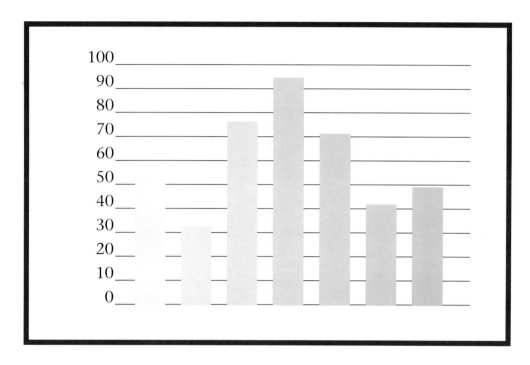

Logos

Whether you are designing a new logo, or using an existing one, logo treatments are not something to be taken lightly. Ideally, an organization's logo will be used for years, or even decades, so it should seldom, if ever, be changed. This way, it builds equity—public recognition. Versatility is important too, because a logo needs to be effective in all sizes, from the smallest ad to billboards or the sides of trucks.

Designing logos

In your work, you may be called upon to design a logo. There are many things to keep in mind as you embark upon a logo assignment:

■ Design for all sizes

Avoid fine lines and intricate illustrations, because they may become obscure when the logo is printed very small, such as on a business card. Pay special attention to any reversed type.

■ Design for all uses

A logo must have the same impact whether it's used in an advertisement or to identify a building. Plan for other uses even if you're designing a company logo for a QuarkXPress newsletter. This means you should make the logo bold and distinctive. It also means that it should look equally good in black and white as it does in color.

■ Keep it simple

Complicated color blends, special inks, obscure fonts—all these can make it difficult when your client wants to reprint letterhead or other materials. You may not be available to guide the client in the future applications of the logo.

■ Avoid trendiness

To ensure that a logo has staying power, don't use trendy colors or typefaces. Those that may have appeal today could look hopelessly dated in just a few years. Strong, primary colors are a good bet, and classic typefaces not only ensure readability, but also lend an air of solidity to the logo.

■ Make it proportional

A logo should not be noticeably horizontal or vertical, because that may restrict its uses. For example, if a long horizontal logo needs to be placed into a tall, thin advertisement, it will need to be sized smaller to keep its proportion. Seeing if it fits into a circle or square is a good test for proper proportions. As a rule of thumb, don't exceed a 1:2 ratio in either direction (twice as wide as tall, or twice as tall as wide).

■ Design as a unit

When logos are created in a graphics program they can be exported as a single piece. Programs such as Aldus FreeHand or Adobe Illustrator are ideal for creating logos. This allows for easy re-sizing in page layout applications, and avoids such problems as point size in relation to graphic elements and letter spacing.

■ Typographical treatments

If a client does not wish to use a graphic, you can still create a distinctive typographical logo. It is very important to pay attention to kerning, linespacing and other typographical concerns. It is also important to create such a logo in a program other than QuarkXPress if possible.

■ Build upon equity

If you are designing a new logo, try to use elements of the old one to establish continuity.

Using existing logos

Organizations are understandably concerned about their logos and how they are used. As a designer, you must never take liberties with your client's identity.

■ Ask for a style manual

If you're doing work for a large company, they probably have a corporate style manual which will tell you the appropriate use of their logo. It will also contain the proper PMS colors.

■ Don't crowd the logo

Design so that the logo stands alone, surrounded by plenty of white space. Make sure it's appropriately large relative to other visual elements on the page.

■ Don't use the logo as a graphic

Resist the temptation to use the company's logo as a screened background with text on top of it. Similarly, don't use the logo as part of some other graphic, such as superimposed over a photograph. Always treat it as a stand-alone element.

■ Never redraw a logo

Don't redraw a company's logo or reset it in type, no matter how simple it may look. There may be subtle nuances you are not aware of, and it will only cause your client distress if you miss them. Instead, ask for a photostat or electronic file of the logo. If unavailable, ask the client to carefully review your recreated version of the logo.

■ Use the logo as a starting point

If the logo will be featured prominently in your design, you can use its colors, typefaces, and other forms as elements in your publication. This will lend an air of cohesiveness to your document.

GRAPHICS

141

Transforming

After locating, converting and importing graphics, they can be transformed to polish their appearance. QuarkXPress enables you to resize, stretch, crop, skew, rotate, and reflect graphics with ease and control.

Cropping Graphics

Imported graphics sometimes need to be cropped to eliminate areas you don't want to print. It is important to crop images in the application in which they were created if possible before you import them because QuarkXPress will keep all the file information and process it during output even if it has been cropped from view.

If you cannot crop in the original program, you can use the Cropping tool in QuarkXPress. Here are some points to remember:

■ Objects can only be cropped at right angles; to "crop" on a diagonal, position a paper filled rectangle over the image and rotate the rectangle appropriately.

■ If something you wish to crop from a graphic appears in the middle of a photo or line art, you may have to use one or more polygons with fills. You can go to a 400% size view to position these polygons accurately.

■ To save time and eliminate unnecessary keystrokes, always use a corner handle when cropping; this way, you change two measurements at once.

Crop effectively

Prominently featuring *part* of a photo or illustration is often more effective than using the entire photo. Decide what it is in the graphic that contains the most important information or will prove most enticing to the reader, and crop out the rest. Here's how to crop a photo or graphic:

1. Select the graphic to be cropped.

2. Position your cursor over one of the handles.

3. Crop out all of the unwanted elements by repostioning one or all of the handles.

4. After you have the correct proportions for the image, you can click on the center of it, and turn your cursor into a grabber hand which moves the image around inside the borders of the crop as you move the mouse.

Resizing Graphics

When resizing graphics always hold the Shift+Option+Command keys down when moving a handle to ensure that the graphic retains its original proportions. In addition, keep these things in mind when resizing a graphic:

■ If part of the graphic is already aligned correctly, (for example, a left top corner of the graphic fits in the left top corner of a column) use the handle opposite (in this case, the right bottom corner) to resize the graphic, so you won't have to realign it.

■ If a scan is going to be significantly reduced from its size in the original placed file, consider reducing it in the program where it was created. (For example, reducing an image size in Photoshop will make a significantly smaller file size, making imagesetting go faster.)

■ If a scan is going to be increased dramatically in size, you may end up with a blurred, highly-pixillated image with poor resolution. There is nothing you can do if an image began small, or a scan's file size was reduced. In this case, you should not use the graphic in any size greater than 150% of its original size.

■ When resizing a rectangle drawn in QuarkXPress where it is important to keep the proportions, it's almost automatic that you'll hold the Shift key and watch your rectangle become a square. Using the Measurements palette instead is the easiest way to resize a rectangle. (See Measurements Palette, page 62.)

The self-promotion piece to the left shows the use of many different graphic elements, some of which have been transformed by stretching, skewing, and rotating.
Design: Bay Graphics, Berkeley, CA

143

Distort the image

QuarkXPress features enable you to distort and manipulate images. Stretched, rotated, reflected, and distorted images give a modern look to your publication—probably because they draw attention to the fact that a computer was used in its creation. In addition to giving an interesting look to good graphics, distortion can be used to compensate for low-quality original artwork.

Here are some ways to give graphics a distorted, abstract appearance:

- Stretch the image until pixellation becomes obvious.

- Stretch more in one direction than another. This works best if the stretch is so dramatic as to be very obvious.

- Stretch, and rotate the graphic.

- Increase contrast dramatically to posterize images. (This only works on black and white, paint-type, and grayscale TIFF images.)

- Print the graphic in a second color, perhaps as a negative image.

- Copy and Step and Repeat a graphic over itself. Crop away part of the top layer. Make the top image a negative image or use another color to set it apart from the other.

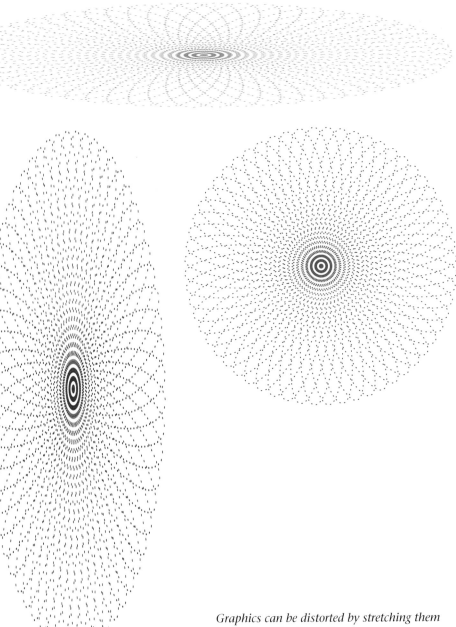

Graphics can be distorted by stretching them vertically or horizontally.

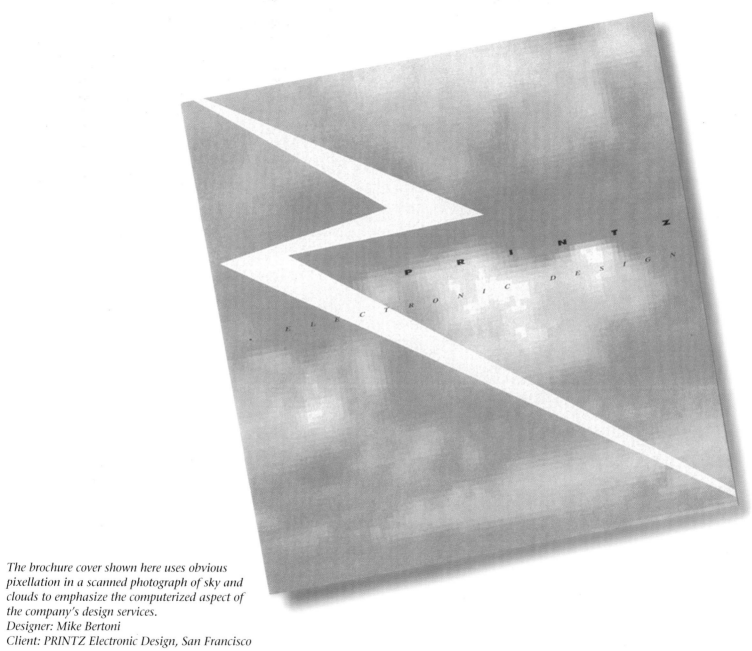

The brochure cover shown here uses obvious
pixellation in a scanned photograph of sky and
clouds to emphasize the computerized aspect of
the company's design services.
Designer: Mike Bertoni
Client: PRINTZ Electronic Design, San Francisco

Transforming your image...

The style menu is used to change the appearance or printing characteristics of paint-type and grayscale TIFF images. You can use these options on any imported TIFF file without worry, because if you make choices which you later decide are wrong, you can click Reset to revert to the previous settings.

You can print an image as a grayscale, halftone with dots, or a line pattern. If you choose to print it as a halftone, you can indicate the frequency of dots, which is dictated by the printing method being used, and if you're using a line screen for special effects, you can choose the angle of the lines.

Special effects

If your project is to be printed in one or two colors only, you can achieve a wide range of effects using this tool.

- Increase the contrast to reduce the number of levels of gray. This will posterize any image, reducing it to its essential information.

- Use a coarse line screen, or change the angle of the line screen to abstract an image.

- Lighten the image so that it can be printed under text or other graphics.

Normal Contrast *Negitive* *High Contrast*

Posterized *Other Contrast* *Line Screen*

Setting line screens

TIFF or PICT images can be assigned the correct line screen for optimal reproduction, before your document is sent for high-resolution imagesetting. This is accomplished with individual images placed into your file—or this can be done globally when you go to print. If you want to run your whole job at a particular line screen, choose Page Setup and enter the LPI in the entry field. Regardless of what resolution your image was scanned and saved at, you must still assign a line screen value if you are going to print it as a halftone. Not doing so risks that the image will be set at a coarser line screen than is desirable.

- If you are using a photocopier for your final duplication, you want to assign no more than an 85 line screen.

- If you are using offset printing for your final duplication and your printer is using paper plates rather than metal plates, set the line screen at no more than 120 LPI.

- If your printer is using metal plates for high quality offset printing, choose a line screen of 133 to 150 (or higher, if your printer is capable of the highest quality).

- Always include the line screen as part of the file information with any order you place to a service bureau for high-resolution imagesetting.

The graphic above is created by placing a TIFF scan, exactly on top of another. Next use the style menu to create a negative of the image. Crop down to reveal part of the original graphic underneath.

This graphic uses the same principles outlined above, but each scan is printed in a different color rather than a positive or negative.

GRAPHICS

Borders

Creating Borders

It's very useful to be able to draw a line around or place a background behind a graphic quickly and with precision This menu simplifies the task, and allows for precision.

For Borders... to work best, it is important to perform your photo cropping, sizing, rotation and skewing before applying.

1. Select the graphic you wish to have a border. In the example here, a grayscale TIFF scan has been changed to black and white so that it will become transparent, allowing the red background to show through.

2. Choose Frame... from Item menu.

3. Indicate the number of points you wish the border to be outside the graphic in the dialog box.

4. Select the Color palette to specify background color and tint.

148

The photo of the earth as seen on this holi-
day card, was transformed by using the
Other contrast feature within the Style
menu... A gradient fill goes from full-strength
blue to white on the inside of the card.
Designer: Michael J. Nolan
Client: Film & Video Service, San Francisco

Gradient fills

Gradient fills imitate nature's light as found in sunsets and shadows, and add drama and depth to your publication. You can create gradient fills in QuarkXPress by setting your choice of color from the color palette. Select the first color for the background, then the second. You also have the option to select percentages and amount of rotation for each.

Uses for gradient fills

Because of the ease of creating them in electronic publishing programs, gradient fills have become very popular—almost to the point of overuse. If handled well, they can be a beautiful addition to any document. Keep these things in mind when using them:

- Gradient fills are a good substitute for screened rectangles under text. You should follow the rule about keeping them light if they will be placed underneath text. To ensure readability, unless the screen is a very light color, it is not advisable to make a fill which goes from 100% to 0% and place text on it: the text would have to be reversed against the 100% and solid on the lighter part.

- You can create the appearance of a bleed without incurring the expense of trimming your pages by using gradient fills that blend to white as they reach the edge of the page.

- One or more gradient fills placed atop of each other can be very effective.

Imported gradients

Gradient fills can be created as blends in programs such as FreeHand, Illustrator, or Photoshop. They can be set up as black and white or color blends. Here are some considerations when using them in QuarkXPress:

- There is the possibility of stepping or banding when using gradient fills, evidenced by jumping from one shade to the next visibly. Generally, the higher the resolution of your output, the less banding will be a problem.

- You cannot create high-quality gradient fills for use on a laser printer: banding is unavoidable.

- Gradient fills created in another software program can be imported into QuarkXPress and can be stretched or cropped. You must be careful, however; if you stretch a 1" original blend to a width of 3" or 4", the blend steps get larger. Sometimes this can result in the steps becoming visible.

Gradients without software

You can still produce gradient fills even if you do not have a scanner, drawing program, or other software to create them. It is possible to purchase self-adhesive sheets made by Letreset, Zipatone, or other manufactures in art supply stores, and either paste them into your camera ready art boards or provide them to your printer for stripping into film. They come in several dot sizes, with variable gradations.

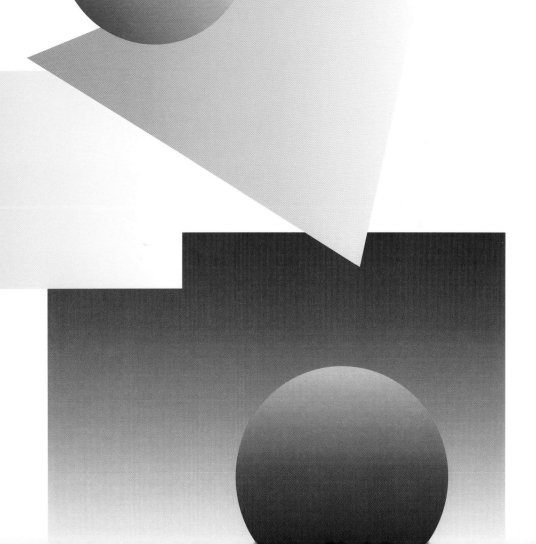

Links

Linking graphics files to your QuarkXPress document simplifies production. You can reduce publication size by building links to the files it contains, and at the same time provide for automatic updating should those source files be changed.

Because QuarkXPress assembles files from numerous different programs in various file formats, it needs to maintain a link to the originals in order to prevent the publication from including all the data in the individual files.

Links

When you place text or a graphic, QuarkXPress automatically establishes a link to the original document.

Having graphics update automatically can be very useful. When a graphic is changed after it has been placed into a QuarkXPress file, the changes usually reflect a refinement that is desired: new information in a sales graph, color correction on a photograph, and so on. As long as the original size and proportions of the graphic have not changed, the link can be updated automatically and the revised graphic will retain all sizing, cropping, and other attributes that were assigned to it when it was first placed into Quark.

To make elements update, choose Picture Usage... under the Utilities menu. Select an item and click on the Update button. Quark will then display a dialog box asking you to locate the original to reestablish the link.

Picture Usage			
Name	**Page**	**Type**	**Status**
Production #16A:scans:Morla marbles	115	TIFF	OK
Production #16A:scans:illust wave.z	116	EPS	OK
Production #16A:scans:fish scan	116	TIFF	OK
Production #16A:scans:woman scan	119	EPS	OK
Production #16A:scans:wall	119	TIFF	OK
Production #16A:scans:Photo055	119	TIFF	OK
Production #16A:scans:Jackson.z	120	TIFF	OK
Production #16A:scans:Jackson.z	120	TIFF	OK
Production #16A:scans:Jackson.z	120	TIFF	OK

Update   Show Me

A QuarkXPress publication that is output and printed with minimal difficulty is the objective of the designer. The pages which follow contain information about files, output, and the printing process. Knowing as much as you can about these steps will enable you to make the right decisions for your layout.

Files

The maintenance and organization of electronic data files is the basis of all electronic publishing. It's sometimes frightening to realize that all your work on a given project is really nothing more than a series of lines of code represented by 0s and 1s. This makes it imperative to create QuarkXPress files that you and others can work with.

Storage and compression

File storage and compression are two of the most important issues confronting electronic publishers. Today's inexpensive storage media and faster, more effective ways to compress file sizes make complex data files possible—and usable.

QuarkXPress files can become very large, very fast, because QuarkXPress assembles data files generated in other programs. A full-color TIFF scan can contain many megabytes of information. When you place several scans into your document along with EPS and text files, the QuarkXPress file can very quickly exceed the capacity of your available storage media. QuarkXPress helps alleviate this situation by enabling you to link images to a publication.

If floppy disks can't hold your file, you will need to consider other forms of storage media to transfer files to service bureaus for output. Other storage media available include SyQuest cartridges (44 or 88 megabyte removable disks) or optical disks (600 megabyte removable cartridges) written to and read by special disk drives.

Compression programs such as Disk Doubler by Fifth Generation Systems, Inc. and StuffIt Deluxe by Aladdin Systems, Inc. condense file size. These programs encode files so that they take up less space on disks. Sometimes a compression program can reduce a file to less than half of its original size. Compression programs are invaluable for sending large QuarkXPress files over modems to service bureaus or printers. Using a compression program can sometimes mean that a floppy disk is adequate to hold your file.

Generally, these products include a decompression program which you can distribute freely so that you can send compressed files to others without worrying about whether they have the program or not. It is also possible to create what is called a self-extracting file, which decompresses automatically when it's double-clicked. However, these files are larger by necessity than the smallest compressed files.

Saving

When working with QuarkXPress files (or any files for that matter) it is essential to have backup copies because files can be accidentally deleted or even damaged. Many production departments are networked and backup takes place to a storage device on a nightly basis. Even this may not be often enough to make backups, especially if your working file is damaged at the end of a full day's work, before backup. My own rule of thumb to make a backup copy after every four hours of work—and more often than that when a deadline is drawing near. Make backups of scans and other graphics files as well, because they too can become damaged.

It is important to establish work practices that are consistent and leave no room for doubt about which file is a backup and which is the current working file. It's sensible to keep current working files on your hard drive and make backup copies to floppy disks, SyQuest, or optical cartridges, or to the network server.

Here is a system of making backup files that will also compact the document size:

1. Save the file at the point that you want to make a backup. After the save is complete, request Save as... from the File menu.

2. Keep the same name for the file, but type .bu as an extension to the file name, and save it to the hard drive on which you are working.

3. After the Save as... is complete, close the file. Copy it to the disk you're using for backup by dragging its icon from the local drive onto the backup disk.

4. Open the backup file, and do another Save as... onto the backup disk, deleting the .bu from the name, so the file has its original name.

5. Close the second copy on the backup disk, and manually copy it to the original local drive. (You will know you have the correct name and location if you get a query as to whether you want to replace an older file with the same name. If you do not get this query, you have misnamed or mislocated your file copy.) The Save as... process usually makes the file substantially smaller, and you now have a backup copy should your working file become damaged.

Organization and naming

If you do a large amount of work for the same client, or have several related projects going on at the same time, file and folder organization and naming can be organized as follows:

1. Create a master folder on your hard drive with a job number, followed by the client or project name. (An easy way to assign job numbers is by a six digit process beginning with year, followed by month, and then by the numerical order of the job. For example, the second job in April of 1994 would be numbered 940402.)

2. Inside the master folder, create three other folders: Text (if you are receiving word-processed files for placement into your publication), Graphics (to hold scans, screen captures, and other art files), and Final, (to hold your current working QuarkXPress publication(s).

3. Place text and graphics files in the proper folders, and save working files to the Final folder. Use job numbers in the file names if you wish (to facilitate finding the files later when revisions need to be made).

4. As you complete projects, archive them to backup media. Storing them on your hard drive after they are completed can be a waste of disk space, and will slow down processing time for your CPU.

5. You can create a database in a program such as FileMaker Pro including information such as job number, date, file names, commercial printer, color numbers, and so forth to keep track of where these files are located and the necessary information about them.

Printers

The destination printer for your files determines many design and production decisions. From a flyer printed on a laser printer, to a full-color brochure requiring high-resolution imagesetting, understanding your printing options will help you determine the best way to accommodate your printer in your design work.

Dot Matrix printers

Dot matrix printers should be used for final output of low-end publications such as personal correspondence and the like. Resolution from a dot matrix printer is not adequate to justify the cost of any reproduction method other than photocopy.

Inkjet printers

In terms of quality, inkjet printers are better than dot matrix, but not as good as laser printers. Though their resolution is sometimes comparable to or higher than that of laser printers, the method used for placing the dots on the page is less precise.

Inkjet printers are useful for producing color proofs, but are not recommended for documents to be reproduced by the offset printing process.

Laser printers

Laser printers were crucial in the desktop publishing revolution. Many people believe that all desktop published documents are laser printed: most are proofed on a laser printer, and some never go beyond laser printer stage.

Laser printers have lower resolution than imagesetters. The resolution of most laser printers is 300 dots per inch (DPI), although some can achieve output as high as 1,000 DPI. The higher the DPI, the sharper the type and images in your publication.

Laser prints are not generally used as camera ready art for offset printing. Because of their low resolution, they print acceptable announcements, flyers, letters, and other such projects. The fact that they cannot print to the edge of a page means that bleeds are not possible (unless you're printing a letter-sized page on a printer capable of tabloid sized output).

Color laser printing

Color laser technology has yielded some very high-end color printers that can be used for both proofing and to produce the final printed piece, especially for signs or posters that will be produced in limited quantities. Many companies are now offering color copiers that you can combine with a raster image processor (RIP) that outputs high-quantity color Macintosh documents. Current limitations of this technology include low resolution, small page size and inability to print a two-sided page. These limitations are being rapidly addressed by manufacturers, and in the future you can expect to see many laser printed color publications, that were never output to film or plate.

Oversize printing

For creating signs, posters, oversize proofs and comps, many service bureaus offer large format printers that output PostScript files at very large sizes—measured in feet, not inches. Although color quality is not outstanding, the technology should improve steadily until this method becomes an accepted standard for the creation of signs. Look for output under such names as Cactus or Megachrome when contacting service bureaus.

Imagesetters

When there's talk of high resolution film or positive output, it's usually about "Lino." This refers to the Linotronic imagesetter built by the Linotype-Hell Corporation, a standard, along with other brands of high-resolution printers such as Agfa Compugraphic and Varityper. These printers are capable of output over 3,000 DPI, and are usually only found in large companies or service bureaus because of their cost.

Imagesetter output can usually be purchased from service bureaus for a few dollars per letter size page. It can be ordered either on paper or film (positive or negative). There are a number of things to know about ordering high-resolution imagesetting, which are covered in the Service Bureaus section, page 165.

QuickDraw & PostScript

To produce graphic shapes for monitors and printers, the Macintosh uses a programming language called QuickDraw. If outputting to a Post-Script or PostScript compatible printer, the page image must be converted from QuickDraw to PostScript. This requires a printer driver—a software file that converts to the proper printer language.

PostScript, a page description language developed by Adobe Systems, has become the standard for printing pages composed on personal computers. Printer manufacturers license the software from Adobe for their PostScript printers. Some printers, called PostScript clones, have interpreters that emulate PostScript code, but this does not always work flawlessly.

You can save QuarkXPress files in pure PostScript code which can then be sent to the printer without requiring a print driver to convert the file from QuickDraw.

PostScript printer description files (PPDs)

PPDs are only used for PostScript printers. They come with QuarkXPress, and you select the ones to add to your System folder when you install QuarkXPress. There is no need to install PPDs for printers you do not have. Each PPD contains detailed information about a specific printer including paper sizes, default fonts, optimized screen angles, and more. QuarkXPress uses PPDs to efficiently print to specific printers.

PostScript and TrueType fonts

The Macintosh uses both TrueType and PostScript fonts.

PostScript fonts are made up of two parts: bitmapped fonts and the printer font file. The bitmapped fonts are used for screen display, and the printer font files are interpreted by the printer to produce a proper typeface.

TrueType is Apple's System 7 font solution used to display scaled typefaces without the jagged edges often seen onscreen. They also allow non-PostScript printers to print the typefaces at any size while maintaining their sharp images.

When QuarkXPress files are sent for imagesetting, use of TrueType fonts can produce unpredictable results.

Downloading fonts

When you use a font that is not installed in your laser printer, the Macintosh must download the PostScript font file to the printer. This takes time, and can significantly slow down the printing process. If there is a font that you will use often, download that font to your printer using the font downloader that comes with the font package. You cannot do this with too many fonts, however, because your printer has limited memory.

It is possible in many cases to attach an additional hard drive to a printer and download additional fonts to that drive so the printer can use it as memory.

Printer utilities

- **Adobe Type Manager (ATM)**
- **Adobe Type Reunion**
- **Suitcase**

Printing PostScript to disk

This is a method of creating a file for output if the output system does not have QuarkXPress, or for creating "snapshots" of individual pages or page spreads for inclusion into a QuarkXPress or other document.

If you do wish to perform this function for sending a complete file for output, it is done simply, using the Print dialog box.

1. Choose Save Page as EPS the File menu.

2. Make all selections, such as page numbers to be printed, scale, color, and so forth.

3. Name the file and select its location.

4. Click Save.

To save a file as a PostScript graphic, such as the reduced page displayed here, you need to select Save Page as EPS under the File menu. It will then display a dialog box where you are to input the page and percentage for the final output.

Printers

QuickDraw & PostScript

To produce graphic shapes for monitors and printers, the Macintosh uses a programming language called QuickDraw. If outputting to a Post-Script or PostScript compatible printer, the page image must be converted from QuickDraw to PostScript. This requires a printer driver—a software file that converts to the proper printer language.

PostScript, a page description language developed by Adobe Systems, has become the standard for printing pages composed on personal computers. Printer manufacturers license the software from Adobe for their PostScript printers. Some printers, called PostScript clones, have interpreters that emulate PostScript code, but this does not always work flawlessly.

You can save QuarkXPress files in pure PostScript code which can then be sent to the printer without requiring a print driver to convert the file from QuickDraw.

PostScript printer description files (PPDs)

PPDs are only used for PostScript printers. They come with QuarkXPress, and you select the ones to add to your System folder when you install QuarkXPress. There is no need to install PPDs for printers you do not have. Each PPD contains detailed information about a specific printer including paper sizes, default fonts, optimized screen angles, and more. QuarkXPress uses PPDs to efficiently print to specific printers.

PostScript and TrueType fonts

The Macintosh uses both TrueType and PostScript fonts.

PostScript fonts are made up of two parts: bitmapped fonts and the printer font file. The bitmapped fonts are used for screen display, and the printer font files are interpreted by the printer to produce a proper typeface.

TrueType is Apple's System 7 font solution used to display scaled typefaces without the jagged edges often seen onscreen. They also allow non-PostScript printers to print the typefaces at any size while maintaining their sharp images.

When QuarkXPress files are sent for imagesetting, use of TrueType fonts can produce unpredictable results.

Downloading fonts

When you use a font that is not installed in your laser printer, the Macintosh must download the PostScript font file to the printer. This takes time, and can significantly slow down the printing process. If there is a font that you will use often, download that font to your printer using the font downloader that comes with the font package. You cannot do this with too many fonts, however, because your printer has limited memory.

It is possible in many cases to attach an additional hard drive to a printer and download additional fonts to that drive so the printer can use it as memory.

Printer utilities

■ Adobe Type Manager (ATM)

■ Adobe Type Reunion

■ Suitcase

160

This "snapshot" of the facing page was saved as an EPS graphic by writing Postscript to disk, and importing into the Quark file. It was reduced in size and had both the border and drop shadow added in Quark.

Service bureaus produce high resolution imagesetting of your electronic files. This enables you to provide camera-ready art to a commercial printer. The key to working successfully with a service bureau is to exchange information about their policies, prices, turnaround time, software and hardware, and specifics about your material.

Range of services

Service bureaus offer different services—most of which center around high-resolution imagesetting. Some are open 24 hours a day with self-service workstations to create or polish your files, then print to laser printers or imagesetters. These service bureaus often include access to scanners and color printers, and on-site high volume photocopying. Other bureaus do not offer this kind of direct customer involvement, and specialize in high-end scanning, color proofs, and imagesetting supervised by well-trained and knowledgeable staff—usually at a higher cost per page. If you have not worked with scanning or imagesetting before, it is probably best to use a full service shop. As you become more familiar with the processes, self-service may become a viable alternative for you.

Some companies opened from the onset of electronic publishing throughout the late 1980s. Others evolved as expanded services from traditional typesetting or prepress houses. The latter is usually better for high-end color publishing requirements because they have more experience in traditional typography and color separation standards, and use a traditional method when it makes sense to do so. A newer, Mac-oriented shop will do just fine for simpler jobs.

Scheduling

Electronic publishing is a deadline-driven business. Both self- and full-service shops are often hectic places with a high level of activity. For this reason, it may be unrealistic to expect them to drop everything else to meet your deadline when you need a few pages of imagesetter output immediately. Build service bureau turnaround time into your deadline and budget. Many companies can accommodate quick turnaround with 1-hour, 2-hour or 8-hour service—and charge from double to quadruple for doing so. Your deadline may require rush service and you must be prepared to pay for it.

Make appointments at self-service shops, and build in time for things to go wrong, because they often do. Alert full-service shops to when they can expect to receive your files, how many pages you'll be printing, and when you need them. Again, even with full-service output, build in time for mistakes, because they can happen.

Before sending files

Never send your original file. Make a copy of it and send the copy.

Never send a file for imagesetting until you have seen a final laser proof. Skipping this simple step can cost you frustration and money. Send laser proofs of each page with your order. Someone running imagesetter output late at night has no way of knowing if what's being imaged is correct, unless there's a laser print with which to compare it.

If you cannot get your laser printer to print a file, don't send it to a service bureau and expect them to "fix" it. This will cause them to waste time, and they may charge you. If you can't get your file to print, don't make the assumption that they will be able to.

Make sure your file is exactly the way it needs to be. Service bureaus are very reluctant to open your files and make changes to them. Do not ask them to do so, unless you have a long-standing relationship with the company and know their capabilities.

Transport media

The enormous file sizes of many Quark projects often makes the traditional floppy disk unworkable when transmitting files for imagesetting.

If you use a file compression program such as StuffIt Deluxe or Disk Doubler, make sure that your service bureau has the specific program you're using, and can un-compress your file. Otherwise, be sure to send a self-extracting file.

When sending a SyQuest disk or optical cartridge, make sure that the service bureau has a drive to handle your removable disk. Put the files you want to have output into a readily visible folder, containing the name of the bureau and today's date. Don't send a disk with other valuable original files on it, unless they are backed up. These disks are very expensive, so clearly label them with your name, address and telephone number.

This order form from Octagon Graphics of San Francisco shows how many questions must be answered when ordering imagesetter output.

Modem transmission

Modems are another way to get files to service bureaus. Many shops have computers set aside to receive modem transmissions from their customers, some with easy-to-use bulletin-board interfaces. If your file is really large, you should compress it before sending. If you don't have a compression program, simply let the transmission take as long as it needs—providing you and your service bureau are willing to tie up the phone lines and computers for that long. You can send large files at night after you've left the office, but be aware that if there is a transmission error, you'll return in the morning only to find an interrupted modem transmission message.

Information for service bureaus

Most service bureaus have developed order forms with extensive checklists to deal with the information about particular files and the specific kinds of output customers require. If you do not have one of these checklists, you should still provide this information to your service bureau. (See order form from previous page.) Some of the questions contained on these lists are as follows:

■ File names

The importance of this information is obvious; this is how the service bureau knows what file(s) to image. Be sure to include the names of any necessary linked files, too.

■ File type

The service bureau needs to know which software program and what version of the program you have used in creating your file(s).

■ Page size and orientation

The service bureau needs to know whether your file is letter size, tabloid size or larger to provide the proper output.

■ Output characteristics

The output you need is specified here. Do you want film or paper, positive or negative, emulsion up or down?

■ Line screens

Whether you are providing your printer with film negative or positive output, you must be aware of the line screen requirements. Many service bureaus will provide a default line screen of 90 or 100 if you do not specify.

■ Linked files

If you have included linked graphics in your publication, electronic files of those graphics must be provided so that the data contained in them is available to QuarkXPress for the final output process. It is your responsibility to make sure that all files are provided and properly linked to the images in your publication. You must also assign line screen values for any grayscale TIFF images, or they will not print properly.

■ Fonts

Knowing the fonts contained in a file is crucial for the service bureau, for the same fonts must be on the system that outputs your page(s). You must indicate all fonts used (don't forget Zapf Dingbats, fonts used in logos or graphics, or other incidental fonts). If the service bureau does not have the fonts you've used, send along electronic files of screen and printer fonts for them.

Utilities are beginning to appear that claim to create suitable substitute fonts for output by matching the closest available font and changing its characteristics to approximate those you originally used. This might be useful in a pinch, but in general, should be avoided.

Compiling file information

Few frustrations in electronic publishing are worse than finding a Yen sign where you expected bullets because of a font substitution on twenty four pages of imagesetter film. A mistake like this usually requires re-running all the film at rush rates. Fortunately, there is an easy and automatic way to compile most of the information a service bureau needs about your file. By selecting both the Font Usage and Picture Usage options from the Utilities menu you can get a quick overview of all the fonts used within your publication as well as the location and current status of all of the art which has been used.

Service bureau equipment

Electronic prepress service bureaus are built around output of high-resolution imagesetting. Using the Linotronic imagesetter as an example, this is what high-resolution equipment consists of:

■ Raster image processor (RIP)

The RIP is the heart of the system. It is a computer with a very fast CPU and a large amount of memory. It contains the PostScript interpreter that converts PostScript code to the high resolution bitmap needed by the imaging recorder.

■ Imaging recorder

This is the part of the imagesetter that actually prints onto the film or paper. The feed mechanisms of these recorders must be very precise to maintain registration for each printout.

■ Processor

After the film or paper inside the imagesetter is printed, it must be processed. This is similar to developing film from cameras; it requires a darkroom process to create the image. Service bureaus that regularly clean and calibrate their developers offer better quality, and this is something about which you should inquire.

Other equipment

Your service bureau may have some of the following equipment:

■ Scanners

Scanners can be black and white or full color, with resolution up to 1,200 DPI or more. Some, such as the Barneyscan enable you to scan slides or transparencies, and others can scan line art and continuous tone photographs. Drum scanners are high-end equipment requiring art to be attached to a drum that spins as the scanning takes place. If you send art to a service bureau to be scanned, be sure to specify resolution, file type and format. Make sure art you send is well-protected and labeled, and send along enough disk storage to contain the scans that are sent back to you.

Some service bureaus offer scanners equipped with optical character recognition (OCR) software that converts printed or typewritten text into a word-processing file that can be edited on your computer and placed into QuarkXPress.

■ Color proofing systems

Color proofs can be very useful when checking the quality of the color, and verifying separations. Some color printers, such as the IRIS or Canon Color Laser printers image directly from your file. Others, such as 3M MatchPrint or DuPont Chromalin use the actual film separations for generating color proofs.

Types of output

Speak to your commercial printer to find out what type of output is required for your project. It will fall into these categories:

■ Paper output

High resolution paper output of your files can be used when reproducing by photocopy, for proofing purposes, for instances when you will be physically pasting artwork onto the boards before submitting them to a commercial printer, and for offset printing. When you provide paper output to a printer, it is still necessary to shoot film from the art, resulting in another generation, and subtle degradation of type and art.

■ Film output

For commercial printing you almost always want film output because it provides the clearest, sharpest printing. There are some difficulties when working with film—especially negatives, to be aware of. One of the most difficult areas concerns final proofing. Everything is a reverse, and what's supposed to print black displays clear. This can be confusing, especially when reversed type and/or gray tones are involved. About the only way to proof negatives is to use a light table, or tape them up on a window.

You need to know whether to provide film positives or negatives. Usually, negatives are the correct choice, but this is a matter to be discussed with your printer. Also ask whether emulsion side should be up or down.

Aldus has two programs that work with QuarkXPress to produce output. They are TrapWise and PressWise.

Aldus TrapWise

Trapping is a color printing process that compensates for potential misregistration as the paper passes through a printing press. Without trapping, printed output may have slight gaps between color elements allowing the underlying paper stock to show through. With trapping, however, the edges of color objects are enlarged or reduced just enough to cover any gaps that may occur.

TrapWise automatically produces these traps by applying appropriate spreads and chokes to objects in color-conforming EPS files. Such files are generated by PostScript-language applications such as QuarkXPress, Aldus FreeHand, PageMaker and Adobe Illustrator.

Once processed through TrapWise, the resulting EPS pages can be output to a PostScript compatible device, including imagesetters, platesetters, and printing presses.

TrapWise handles complex trapping situations such as graduated fills, very small text, and several intersecting colors. It is designed for use by professionals in service bureaus, prepress houses, commercial print shops, in-plant production departments, and publishing operations. It is not intended for the average QuarkXPress user.

Aldus PressWise

Imposition is the arrangement of pages for printing in a press form so that they will appear in correct order when the printed sheet is folded and trimmed. Aldus PressWise is an advanced page-imposition program that enables prepress operators, to automatically prepare multipage documents for printing, folding, and binding in the correct page order. Professional film strippers and production artists use PressWise to design templates for specific imposition needs.

PressWise has automated features to convert the pages of a PostScript file created in QuarkXPress into precise signature forms.

A good way to understand imposition is to actually take a sheet of paper, fold it, number it and make up an eight-page signature as pictured below:

trim trim

| 13 | 4 |
| 16 | 1 |

| 10 | 7 |
| 6 | 11 |

trim trim

| 3 | 14 |
| 2 | 15 |

| 9 | 8 |
| 12 | 5 |

The diagram to the left shows how a printed 16-page signature is folded. The diagram above shows the imposition arrangement of the individual pages prior to printing.

Commercial printing

The capabilities of commercial printers can vary more than those of service bureaus. You must find the right printer for any project, balancing criteria such as quality of work, price, turnaround time, and service. It is crucial to know different printers in your area and to build good relationships with them. Their work is the final step in your QuarkXPress projects.

Different capabilities

Commercial printers can be classified by the kind of work they do. Some specialize in high-volume, and they do print runs of at least 50,000 units; others gladly accept low-volume four color runs. Some have huge web presses larger than semi trailers, while others run small sheet-fed presses that can be quickly and easily set up for two or four color sheet fed work. There are quick printers and high quality printers, and everything in between. A quick printer I have used for years has consistently provided low-cost, fast, high-quality full-color work, so you can't make assumptions about capabilities.

Printers are almost always willing to visit your location, talk about their capabilities and show you their work. They also are usually very happy to give you a tour of their facility.

Prepress departments

Some large printing companies maintain full service prepress departments and are capable of taking QuarkXPress files on disk. (Soon, direct-to-plate technology will be perfected that will make film output unnecessary.) Having files output by the printer saves you the expense of using a service bureau. Of course, the printer is going to be much more likely to output files the way they are needed for printing.

By now, most printers are familiar with electronic publishing, and if you work with them from the beginning of a project, they can give you the benefit of their experience and many valuable tips.

Getting quotes

When securing bids or prices for printing, it's important to get quotes from more than one company. If you're working for a client, your client will appreciate (and maybe even require) this thoroughness. It can be time consuming, so it's convenient to use a system that makes the process easy for everyone concerned.

Create a form to be used for printing quotes with fill-in-the-blank information about a specific job. Fill in the form with the specifics for your job, make photocopies and fax the form to different printers for a quote. (Let the printers know it is coming.) This helps the printers to quickly return a quote, in writing, of the cost.

Don't be impatient if it takes a printer two or three days to get a quote back to you. They need to price paper and assess available resources before they can give you an accurate price and turnaround time. For this reason, it is important to get printing quotes and to decide on the printer early in the design process.

Some of the things a printer needs to know about your job are:

- Number of copies
- 1- or 2-sided
- 1-, 2-, or 4-color
- ink coverage (light or heavy)
- bleeds
- finished size
- folds
- trims
- binding
- turnaround time
- type of camera ready art
- paper stock
- die cuts
- foil stamping

Meeting deadlines

Printers are busy people; they are the final step in a process of deadlines. Everyone wants their work printed right away, and people often expect printers to make up deadlines that may have been missed by copywriters, designers, and service bureaus. Printers will work with you on deadlines, but there are certain processes—such as time for ink to dry before work can be folded—that cannot be shortened.

Printers are schedule jugglers. They have expensive equipment that must be kept in operation. When you are going to miss a deadline for getting work to them, it is only fair to give them as much notice as possible. This kind of communication will help in building and maintaining good relationships with printers.

Bluelines, color proofs and press checks

Even if you are working under a tight deadline, it is important not to skip the proofing process at the commercial printing stage. There are several ways for you to proof work before it has been printed.

■ Bluelines

Bluelines are proofs that a printer creates from film before it is made into printing plates. They show the position of all elements, and are usually trimmed and mocked up in the same way as the final document. There is usually a charge for creating a blueline—and it is well worth the cost. You can spot imperfections the printer may miss like scratches and similar irregularities, misalignment or bad trim information. You may also pick up an error you missed when you were proofing film. This gives you a chance to run new film before that error is repeated in 25,000 copies.

■ Color proofs

3M Matchprints or DuPont Chromalins are used to proof process color jobs, to ensure that alignment, color, and all other aspects of the job are correct. While they are relatively expensive, they are cheaper than the cost of re-running an entire job because of a mistake that could have been corrected.

■ Press checks

Press checks are often difficult to schedule; however, they are invaluable, especially for process color runs. At a press check, you can see one of the first pieces run off, and ensure that everything is correct. You can stop the presses if something is wrong; while that's not a pleasant prospect, it's better than rejecting a job after it's printed. There will usually be an extra charge for a press check.

Post-press services

Printing your publication isn't the end of the process at the commercial printer. There are also the issues of binding, trimming, folding, die cutting, packaging, and delivery. Ensure that you build in the time needed for these things to happen. Some specialties, such as die cutting, may be jobbed out to others.

Index

Symbols

G

Get Picture command (File menu), 118, 121, 126
Get Text command (File menu), 87
grabbing frames, video images, 120
gradient
    backgrounds in process color, 39
    fills, 150-151
graphics
    backgrounds, 132-135
    borders, 136-137, 148-149
    captions, 2
    charts and graphs, 138-139
    clip art, 119
    colors in, 131
    commissioned art, 119
    converting to electronic format, 122-125
    cropping, 142
    distorting, 144-145
    EPS line art, 3
    gradient fills, 150-151
    graying out, 60
    grayscale, 146
    halftones, 146
    importing, 126-129
    in brochures, 15
    in calendars, 16
    in menus, 22
    in posters, 25
    in programs for events, 26
    in resumes, 27
    in spot color, 37
    inline, 128-129
    line screens, assigning, 147
    linking, 152-153
    logos, designing, 18
    photographs, 117-118
    previewing before sending to service
        bureaus, 164

process color, 3, 39
reflecting, 65
resizing, 143
rotating, 65
screen captures, 121
sizing, 65
skewing, 65
sources, 116-117
TIFF scans, 2-3
under text, 131
video images, 120
wrapping text around, 130
graphics programs, 124
graphs
    bar, creating, 138-139
    importing, 138
gray, color effects when printing in
    black, 46-47
graying out graphics, 60
grayscale, 146
Greek text, 2, 9
green, effects of, 34
grid, 54
guides, 61
    setting preferences, 60
Gutenberg, Johann, 5
gutters, 3
    for books, 14

H

H&J dialog box, 112
H&Js command (Edit menu), 112
halftones, 7, 146
handheld scanners, 122
hanging indents, 97
headers, running, 3
headings
    in tables, 3, 32
    subheads, 3

headlines, 2
    designing, 88-91
    history, 4
    in advertisements, 12
    in flyers, 21
Helvetica font, 73
Helvetica Narrow font, 73
hierarchies
    for design elements, 6
    for nameplates, 30
    in books, 14
    in flyers, 21
high-resolution equipment at service
    bureaus, 165
horizontal rules, 105
Horizontal Scale command
    (Style menu), 82
hyphenation, 112-113

I

Ibid, Inc. stock photographs, 117
Illustrator (Adobe), 95, 117, 124, 141, 150
The Image Bank stock photographs, 117
image control, 146-147
Image Studio program, 118, 124
ImageClub Graphics fonts, 75
imagesetters, 159
    at service bureaus, 165
imaging recorders at service bureaus, 165
importing
    backgrounds, 133-135
    charts and graphs, 138
    gradient fills, 150
    graphics, 126-129
        for initial caps, 95
    Photo CD images, 118
    styles, 86-87, 107
    tables, 32

word processing programs, importing
  text from, 86
wrappers for self-mailers, 66
wrapping text, 3
    around graphics, 130
    in catalogs, 17

X-Z

XLC files, 124
XLS files, 124
XTensions, 14
    INposition (DK&A), 56
    Sonar TOC (Virginia Systems), 31

yellow, effects of, 34

Zapf Chancery font, 74
Zapf Dingbats font, 74, 98, 101, 137
Zipatone sheets of gradient fills, 151
zooming pages, 61